THRIFT

WELBECK
BALANCE

THRIFT YOUR LIFE

Heidi Ondrak

WELBECK
BALANCE

Published in 2023 by Welbeck Balance
An imprint of Welbeck Non-Fiction Limited
Part of Welbeck Publishing Group
Offices in: London – 20 Mortimer Street, London W1T 3JW &
Sydney – Level 17, 207 Kent St, Sydney NSW 2000 Australia
www.welbeckpublishing.com

Design and layout © Welbeck Non-Fiction Ltd 2023
Text © Heidi Ondrak 2023

Heidi Ondrak has asserted her moral rights
to be identified as the author of this Work in accordance with
the Copyright Designs and Patents Act 1988.

A CIP catalogue record for this book is available from the British Library.

ISBN
978-1-80129-309-9

Typeset by Lapiz Digital Services
Printed in Great Britain by CPI Group (UK) Ltd

10 9 8 7 6 5 4 3 2 1

CONTENTS

AN INTRODUCTION TO A THRIFTY LIFE

This is not an ordinary book purchase, it's an investment – a no-nonsense guide to changing habits to slash your cost of living. A book full of hacks and hustles on how to navigate sudden and unpredictable changes in fortune along with tips on how to adapt your life to fit your budget. I guarantee you will have saved yourself a fair few quid every month by the time you've worked through the chapters. It will teach you resilience, which you can then draw on when you need to navigate hard times, and some cheeky life hacks that no one teaches in schools. Think of it as a modern-day take on *Mrs Beeton's Book of Household Management* – with extra sass.

At the time of writing this in winter 2022/2023, the cost of living crisis had many of us reaching for our pity pot and licking our wounds, while staring forlornly at a dismal bank balance or a gaping overdraft. The crisis is impacting pretty much everyone, and it has hit us hard – and fast. We are all rationing energy and trying to rein in spending, grappling with the biggest rise in inflation in 100 years. It hasn't been a steady increase, it's been more of a frying pan across the face, BOOM – you're skint. We have gone from comfortable to stretched in record times, our heads are spinning and we haven't yet caught up.

But, if we're going to weather the storm, we need to start changing our mindsets and habits – and fast!

LIFE LESSONS

No one teaches thriftiness and the skills needed to audit every area of your life in order to cut your cloth in schools – hence the need for this book. There are of course fabulous sources of information, advice and guidance on where to get the best and latest deals such as the brilliant Moneysavingexpert forum or Which? surveys, but *applying* all of the changes required to thrift your life takes a pinch of planning, a sprinkle of resilience and a final dusting of strategy.

Here, we recognise that life is full of changing fortunes – sh*t happens that you could have controlled better, and then sh*t happens that you have absolutely no control over whatsoever. As with the current cost-of-living crisis. This is the definitive guide on how to pull your belt in when you need to, how to waste less and how to change your habits to save you money without resorting to eating thin gruel and shivering over a candle. It is packed with practical hacks to adapt to life's financial ups and downs.

My tips, hacks and hustles range from the well-versed and practical to the downright cheeky and outrageous; you can pick and choose, try a few ideas, do what suits you. I will help you to build up a toolkit to get you through the crisis, and to help you feel prepared and in control in case of more energy increases, interest rate rises and eye-watering inflation – and to show you can still maintain a fighting spirit and sunny demeanour. Like a pig looking for truffles, you will be sniffing out bargains and ways to save, enjoying the challenge as you go.

We will look at every area of your life that requires you to part with your hard-earned moolah, and offer hacks and hints for shaving a bit off the cost of everything you spend on. I recognise

2

that people might be feeling paralysed with fear and uncertainty and are looking for tangible things they can do to rein in living costs.

This is the stuff that should be on the national curriculum but isn't.

SOMETHING FOR EVERYONE

It's important to enter this with the right mindset, one of stoicism and flexibility. And you can't do it alone, so I will be sharing how to get the whole family on board and enthused about living well for less too.

From people budgeting on benefits, students managing their loans and (if they're lucky) bursaries, kids leaving home for the first time, working families hammered by the cost of living rises, right through to the mortgaged-up-to-the-hilt middle classes whose disposable income has been squeezed. Hell, it might even be useful for aristocrats in 20-bedroom country piles whose heating bills have left them swapping the Jag for a Micra. Most of us have had it pretty good for a long time – we haven't needed to plan, organise and hustle to get through life, and so those all-important skills needed to live comfortably for less have been lost.

We are entering a new age where the ways of living and managing a household for the last 20 years no longer serve us. People across the globe are looking to navigate this new age. And the good news is that all the advice here also helps us to live more sustainably as well as economically. We can feel happy in the knowledge that when we consume less we are naturally "doing our bit" to reduce our carbon footprint and care for the planet, as well as caring for our finances.

At the time of writing...

This book was written during winter, spanning 2022/2023. All prices including in the text are indicative of that time. Energy and food prices will, of course, change and I have provided links to resources to help you calculate the most up-to-date unit costs for energy.

MY THRIFTY LIFE

My life – like many – has been far from linear. I have been church-mouse poor, better off, desperately skint and then better off again. I can relate to everyone: I've been on benefits and I've clawed my way to becoming middle class. I'm a full-time working mum. I have worked hard to gain professional qualifications that meant I was financially comfortable, and then life events have smacked me in the chops and left me living on a strict budget again.

As a council house kid, I grew up in the 1970s in Wolverhampton – we liked to boast that our council estate was the biggest in Europe. Mum and Dad both came from families of 12. My granddad died when my dad was young, so he and his siblings were carted off to an orphanage in Derby. My mum's dad also died when she was young. They both grew up in households where hustling through life to get by was the norm.

"NOT MORE BEANS, MUM!"

Growing up in the seventies, I remember money being tight when my dad was on strike as a General Post Office (GPO) engineer. I have a phobia of baked beans now because of my childhood;

when dad was on strike we dined on beans with such alarming frequency I can't look at a bean now – I have bean-induced trauma! Every single item my mum bought in the weekly grocery shop was necessary. There was none of this walking around the supermarket with a trolley throwing stuff in because it was new, looked nice or you fancied it. Meals were planned and strictly budgeted for. There were limited snacks between meals, and once they were gone they were gone. There was no waste. You got new stuff at Christmas and for birthdays. And, you know what, we were happy, healthy and well-cared for.

The budgeting lessons from my childhood have stayed with me – as has my mum's fond description of me: "If you fell in sh*t, you'd come out smelling of roses." This wasn't because I was a particularly lucky kid, teenager or adult; it's because I possess a rare resilience, stoicism and grit. I have always been able to adapt to change and make the best out of a bad situation. I see challenges as opportunities, and have always been able to find hacks and hustles to get me through the hardest of times with a smile on my face and a spring in my step, usually coming out the other side better for the challenge.

NEVER LEAVE A BARGAIN BEHIND

I have always bought and worn second-hand clothes, and my home is full of bargain gems that I have found. I truly believe that you can live really well and stylishly on a meagre budget. I was always hunting out free and cheap stuff we could do with my kids when they were young, and over the years have honed my ability to live well for less. My kids are also well-trained in being thrifty – if they see something on their way home from school that has been discarded in a back lane, they gleefully tell me they have spotted something that I might be able to reuse.

Which brings us to now.

THE COST OF LIVING CRISIS REALITY

As soon as the cost of living crisis hit in early 2022, I felt a call to arms. I could feel my bank account being squeezed, and I started a plan of action to manage through the crisis without amassing huge debt. I started sharing my love of preloved clothes on Instagram in January 2022, and later started sharing cost of living hacks on TikTok. I am a project manager by day, so the skills from my job in managing risk and opportunity seemed to transfer quite naturally. That, coupled with my thrifty upbringing in seventies Britain created a combination that I felt could really help people, by sharing some of my hacks and hints to live for less. I do believe that my mindset is as essential as my actual bank balance when trying to live for less. Despairing over what you cannot have or can no longer afford will most definitely spiral into defeatism and misery – and that is why this book focuses as much on creating a resilient mindset as on budgeting hacks.

Whenever life takes an unexpected turn, I focus on what I can do to save money. I have learned that almost no problem is insurmountable, and I hope that this book will help you to see how you too can *Thrift Your Life*.

CHAPTER 1

A THRIFTY MINDSET

Life truly is a bumpy old ride. One year you are buying fancy Aesop hand wash in SpaceNK because that is within your means, the next you are darting to grab a yellow sticker damaged bottle Jo Malone dupe in Aldi because you are struggling to pay your energy bills. Both of these products do the same thing, but the shopping experience is very different, as is the way the purchase makes you feel.

"RETAIL THERAPY"

I am an emotional shopper. When I feel like there is a little void in my life and I feel down, when I succumb to self-induced anxiety (it all starts with my own thoughts and perceptions), I seek out a little dopamine (aka the feel-good hormone) fix. This, coupled with poor impulse control, can lead to me "adding to basket" and clicking "buy" before the good monkey on my shoulder can yell "STOP!".

Why am I telling you this when I am meant to be helping you to save money? Well, because I am human, I am flawed, and probably more flawed than your average Joe or Jill. If *I* can change *my* mindset around money, budgeting and spending, then anyone can.

WELL & TRULY INFLUENCED

Here is another confession. In lockdown, I let myself be "influenced". A celebrity Instagram influencer, a fabulously warm and funny lady, a millionaire married to a millionaire, piqued my interest. She would show fabulous hauls from Zara (the cheap stuff to her) mixed with her designer wardrobe, she shared styling tips and hints that she promised would make you feel great. Lockdown was a strange time – boredom, anxiety and human frailty all mixed together to make a bizarre soup – and I had an existential shopping crisis. I bought new clothes online – more than I ever had in the past, more than I needed – and I bought clothes that were the influencer's style rather than my own. I used shopping to numb the lockdown malaise.

Did the purchases make me feel good? Only when I ordered them. How did I feel when the boxes arrived? Honestly, I felt shame. When my relationship with the Yodel man progressed from cheery salutations to first name terms, I knew things had gotten out of hand. What did I do? I sold the clothes online, many of them still new with tags. I sold them on closed Facebook groups. I made connections and chatted with the ladies that were buying my clothes. I got as much of a thrill from selling the clothes – if not more – than from the rush of the initial purchase. I gradually joined up the dots and, with some soul searching, realised it was the grinding loneliness of lockdown that I was trying to fix by shopping in this way. I eventually managed to curb my behaviour by taking the actions in the box below.

How to curb impulse online shopping

- Unfollow any influencers who might have led you to unwise purchases. As gorgeous as their lifestyle may be, they can – irrationally – make you feel that yours is lacking in some way.
- Delete shopping apps from your phone.
- Unsubscribe from retailers' emails, as they are often trying to hook you back in with offers and promotions.
- Unfollow retailer pages on social media.
- When browsing online, do not accept cookies. They are like little footprints that lead the retailer back to you if you have browsed a site; they will then target you on social media to get you to finish a transaction. It's their job to part you from your hard-earned cash.
- Introduce a cooling-off period – take a breath before clicking "buy", and ask yourself if the item in your basket is a "want" or a "need"; is it really the best thing since sliced bread, will your world stop turning if you don't have it?
- Consider making a commitment to only buy second-hand clothes. I did this, and made the commitment public by sharing my journey on Instagram, which made me accountable as I set my Instagram profile to public.

From this experience (and many more), I created a Seven-Step Self-Evaluation process to use when I feel tempted to impulsively purchase something online. This applies to second-hand resale sites too, as the temptation to over-shop lurks at every turn. It can feel justified when you are bagging a bargain on Vinted, but it soon adds up.

MY PRE-PURCHASE SEVEN-STEP SELF-EVALUATION

The purpose of my seven-step process is to identify what emotional drivers and triggers are behind some of your shopping habits. Self-awareness is critical to changing financial behaviours and spending habits that are self-defeating.

Before pressing "Buy It Now", ask yourself the following questions. The answers will reveal any purchasing patterns and/or self-defeating habits...

> **"It can feel justified when you are bagging a bargain on Vinted, but it soon adds up."**

STEP ONE
WHAT TIME IS IT?

What am I doing as I add these items to my shopping basket, whether virtually or in real life? For example, am I scrolling on my phone in the morning, about to go to bed, making dinner?

Identifying regular times suggest you've got into a habit and are more likely to be absent-mindedly shopping. Becoming aware is the first step in becoming more conscious about the way you shop. We are all so used to filling in the very small gaps between tasks with browsing on our phones or nipping to the shops, and this can lead to purchases that we don't really need. If you phone scroll and purchase things just before bed, try reading a book as an alternative way to wind down. If you pop into a particular shop on the way back from work or on a lunch break, become aware of this and replace the activity with something that doesn't involve shopping.

Ask yourself:
What time is it?
What am I doing?
What could I do instead?

STEP TWO
HOW AM I FEELING?

Am I stressed, feeling bored or lonely? Am I feeling sorry for myself? Am I self-sabotaging?

Do you shop when you are feeling out of sorts? Do you nip out for a mooch around your favourite shop to fill time if you are feeling bored? At times of stress or emotional discomfort, are you prone to fixing your feelings with buying things that you don't really need? Are you a master of justifying purchases because you have had a tough week, deserve it and need cheering up? When you are financially stretched do you have "Sod it, you only live once" moments when you completely self-sabotage and buy stuff that you absolutely can't afford which will have financial consequences for you? If you answered yes to any, or all of the above, you are most likely to be an emotional shopper. Finding alternative things to do to lift you out of a funk that are not to your financial detriment are key.

Ask yourself:
How am I feeling?
What could I do instead?

Could I visit or call a friend, hit the gym, nip out for a walk, read a book, watch a great movie?

STEP THREE
DO I WANT IT OR DO I NEED IT?

Is this purchase a necessity, is it for a special occasion, or is it an impulse buy? Am I buying this because I am feeling emotionally unsettled in some way?

This step is intended to stop you in your tracks and make you think about whether you are making a conscious decision to buy something new. Have you broken all of the mugs in your house and need something to drink out of, or has your fancy just been drawn to the novelty of a new set? Do you need another black dress or are the three that you already own enough? Did you actually, consciously plan to make this purchase because there is a real need in your life, or will it bring you hours of unbridled joy or entertainment?

Ask yourself:
Did I consciously plan to make this purchase because I have a real need for this item in my life?
Is this purchase a really good investment as it will bring me ongoing, sustained happiness or entertainment?

STEP FOUR
HOW WILL I FEEL IF I DO NOT BUY THIS ITEM?

Can I live without buying this item, or is it just a fear of missing out on a bargain? Will there be a cavernous gap in my lifestyle if I do not have this particular thing?

(The answer to the latter question is usually a resounding no!) This is a bit of a killer question; you have lived this long without that blogger's favourite face cream or the latest faddy gizmo or gadget, so will your life really fall apart if you don't have it, will there be a huge gap in your lived experience if you don't own it? More often than not, that answer is no.

Ask yourself:
What will happen if I don't buy this?
How will I feel if I don't buy this?

STEP FIVE
HOW MUCH USE WILL I REALLY GET FROM THIS PURCHASE?

Will I wear or use it more than once, am I buying it for the novelty of having something new? Will it be an indispensable, labour-saving kitchen gadget or a practical item of clothing I will get multiple wears from?

It's time to get honest with yourself. Up and down the country tagged or barely worn clothes hang in wardrobes, unused and unloved kitchen gadgets nestle in cupboards and drawers. If you are going to use something rarely, does it really justify owning it? Could you borrow from family or friends on the occasions when you may need a floor-length jewelled gown, a circular saw, a spiralizer or an LED face mask.

Ask yourself:
What will the cost per wear or cost per use of this item be?

STEP SIX
HOW LONG CAN I LIVE WITHOUT IT?

Give yourself a cooling-off period. Ranging from 7 to 21 days (see my 21-day rule in the next chapter if you suffer with payday millionaire syndrome). After a pause, has your burning desire to press "Buy" turned into a gentle simmer? Move to Step 7.

Ask yourself:
Can I park this purchase for a few weeks and then decide whether I really need it?

STEP SEVEN
DO I STILL WANT TO BUY IT?

How have I felt living without having that new, shiny object in my life?

Have you completely forgotten about it and moved onto something else or do you spend every waking moment coveting the goodies in your online basket? Usually at this step I resign myself to the fact that I didn't really need to buy the damn thing in the first place and I was scrolling on my phone through boredom and got caught up in the moment and some clever marketing tactics.

Ask yourself:
Does owning this thing still really matter to me?

SEVEN-STEP SUMMARY

The seven steps are intended to make you a more conscious and considered shopper. We are bombarded with opportunities to buy stuff that we don't need, particularly given the majority of us are permanently attached to smartphones. We are marketed to 24/7, and it's hardly surprising that we occasionally get caught up in the hype. I like to use a journal to note down my responses to the self-enquiry questions in these steps (see the template to get you started).

Starting at Step 1, work your way through the steps. Even the act of starting to challenge yourself may diffuse the need to purchase something. If I am honest, I rarely get beyond Step 4, as asking "How will I feel if I do not buy this item?" usually results in the acknowledgement that I was not really that bothered about it in the first place.

The steps will become second nature in time, but occasionally I still find I need to rein myself in belt and braces and systematically work through breaking the unconscious shopping habit. For example, recently, after my kids had been bickering all day, the car then broke down and I was feeling strung out, stressed and a bit sorry for myself. I sat down with a cup of tea and started to scroll through Instagram. An ad popped up from a high-street store and I spied a gorgeous tiered green dress. I added it to my basket knowing full well the car repair bill was going to clean me out for the month. So, I revisited the steps and acknowledged that I was shopping on my feelings and actually wouldn't get that much wear out of the dress as I wasn't planning on going anywhere fancy and it didn't really match with anything that I already had in my wardrobe. The steps stopped me dead in my tracks.

SEVEN STEPS TO SHOPPING SELF-AWARENESS

This template is also available at the back of the book for you to copy as needed.

This exercise is to be used before you make a rash or impulse purchase. It is essentially a cooling-off tool that will make you more self-aware of your triggers for spending on non-essential items. Getting into the habit of repeating these steps when you are hovering over the "Buy It Now" button in an online shopping basket will equip you with insight into your inner saboteur; it will make you question your purchase and, in time, become second nature.

Answer the following questions as fully as you can, in a notebook or journal:

1	What time is it?
2	How am I feeling?
3	Do I want it or do I need it?
4	How will I feel if I do not buy this item?
5	How much use will I really get from this purchase?
6	How long can I live without it?
7	Do I still want to buy it?

LACK & GRATITUDE

Do you have some food in the fridge, a bed to sleep in and a choice of outfits to wear? If the answer is yes, then you are not lacking. What you have is enough. Now I am not some neo-Marxist, but in a capitalist society people want to sell you stuff to make them a profit. They want to create need where there is no real need, and they want you to compare yourself to people who have lots of "stuff".

This creates a feeling of "lack" – a discontent with what you have and own. This is a peculiar self-perpetuating cycle that can lead to you feeling sorry for yourself and that you "deserve" a payday treat to cheer you up. Hands up if you've ever done the whole payday millionaire thing. You know what I mean: you get paid and decide that you have worked hard so you are going to…

… get that sequin dress that you will probably only wear once, another bottle of perfume, oh yes, and you saw some lovely shoes and you may as well get them at the beginning of the month when you can afford it, but OMG what about the cute jumper for your dog and weren't you thinking of changing the colour scheme of all the cushions in your lounge too?…

Then a week later you're counting the days down to payday again, feeling wretched, feeling like you are trapped in "lack", and craving a shopping high more than ever. The whole cycle starts again as the pent-up feeling of lack drives you to do exactly the same next payday.

TRY SOMETHING DIFFERENT NEXT PAYDAY

How different would your budget for the month feel if you didn't splurge on stuff that you don't need as soon as your wages hit your bank? (See the 21-day habit exercise in Chapter 3.) How different would it feel if you reframed your thinking and found delight in things that are free or that you already have? It sounds cheesy and hyper-wholesome, but getting grateful for what you have already can fill your cup, as much if not more than a payday buy that leaves you skint, feeling like a victim of your own crappy pattern of behaviour and lacking all month.

Start by making a list of things that bring you joy – this is best done when you are in a positive mindset. The Joy List will then serve as a great aide memoire when you are feeling hard done by, or discontent with not having the means to splurge and buy something new. Here is what brings me joy.

MY JOY LIST

- The smell of sandalwood incense
- Sunrise
- A natter with my best friend
- Talking to my mum
- The smell of wet earth in the woods
- My 1970s vintage Crimplene dresses
- My teenagers wanting to spend time with me
- My cats
- An afternoon meditation and a self-care nanna nap
- A self-care skincare ritual

These things are all free and they fill my "frazzled mum" cup. They can quickly reframe my thinking, so when I feel compelled to fix my feelings with a random purchase I can pause and pick something off my Joy List because I already have enough to make me feel happy. If I feel like I am going to die without that new dress from Zara, I reframe this and tell myself I want to wear something that makes me feel great, so I dig out one of my favourite 1970s dresses.

Reverting to your Joy List at moments of consumer weakness gives you a replacement activity when you need it. The things on your Joy List won't cost you a penny. In the time you spent scrolling and adding to a basket shortlist, you could have taken a 10-minute walk outdoors or a meditation, given yourself a face mask and pamper, had a giggle with your teen, or played with your pet cat or dog. So, remember to pause and choose something to do from your Joy List.

GRATITUDE

I am not a supercharged self-help guru. I am, however, someone that needs to practise daily gratitude. Life is hard sometimes: there are kinks in the road, there are humps, hurdles and daily challenges that would have you licking your wounds and counting your battle scars in a jiffy. Practising gratitude, however small, does change your mindset and equip you better to deal with the lemons that life throws at you. There are lots of books and guides on gratitude, but you can also keep it really simple: all you need to do at the beginning of the day is jot down the things that you have in your life to be grateful for.

The cost of living crisis has impacted all of our disposable incomes; it has squeezed us financially and it will leave a lot of us feeling justifiably quite angry and sorry for ourselves. We may have to cut back on heating our homes, on our weekly food shop, on the amount of days out we have, on the amount of treats and gifts that we can buy for ourselves and our loved ones. We may not be able to afford to jet off somewhere sunny on holiday, and we may even need to downsize our home, sell the car, skip meals and turn the heating off.

Writing a daily gratitude list is vital in retaining some perspective when the proverbial hits the fan. There is always *something* that you have to be grateful for, granted it's harder to find it when you feel like you are swimming upstream, but there will be something there. Here is what I am grateful for today.

MY GRATITUDE LIST FOR TODAY

- The sun beaming in through the window.
- The kids are off school so I don't have to do the morning get-out-of-bed routine this week.
- I am fit and healthy.
- My mum and dad are fit and well.
- My fleece snoodie.
- Hot water in my shower.
- I have a lovely best friend who just "gets" me.
- My cats play together and they are the best little floof pals – watching them fills my heart with joy.
- I have food in the fridge and plenty to cook a hearty, filling meal this evening.
- It's a dry, bright day and I can dry my washing outside in the yard.

Keep an exercise book or journal in the kitchen, and when you are drinking your first cuppa jot down your Gratitude List. I promise it makes such a difference to a misery mindset. Sadly, there is always someone far worse off, and accepting that and counting your blessings is the first step toward building some resilience to deal with financial blips.

This may all sound very idealistic, but I promise you I have my moments of "Why me?". During the course of a day, events can knock me off guard and take me by surprise. Resentments and niggles build over the course of the day, and I can end the day feeling less than grateful for my lot. Falling asleep with a head full of whirring bitterness affects my mindset, my energy, pragmatism and acceptance.

"Take time to look for positive moments in what may have felt like a crappy day."

I keep a small journal next to my bed, and before I fall asleep I jot down three things that have happened in the day that make me feel grateful or have filled my cup with joy. Taking time to look for positive moments in what may have felt like a crappy day reframes my mindset and alters my mood to feel more optimistic and resilient.

ACCEPTANCE & ADAPTING

Life isn't a sunny linear path. You don't start your first job and then work your way up on a solid upward trajectory trading cars and houses for better versions, and ultimately ending the game with complete financial freedom and security. Stuff happens: redundancy, divorce, break-ups, babies, health issues, and a whopping great cost of living crisis. A bit like snakes and ladders, a life incident can have you sliding down the board quicker than you can get your bearings. Accepting this and being able to cut your cloth, adapting and flexing your standard of living, is key to adapting to life's kinks in the road.

A lack of acceptance can have you feeling like you have lost control. Consumed and paralysed by self-pity, you can feel hard done by and resentful. A lack of acceptance can impact your grit and resilience.

As I've mentioned, I grew up in the 1970s on a housing estate that was so rough it was a police no-go zone. My grandparents and parents may not have had the little luxuries that we do now, and I am not wishing to go back to those difficult times, but what they did have was that grit and resilience that saw them through the most challenging times. I can so clearly remember my gran looking out of the 19th-floor window of her tower block telling me it was the best view in the world. She had very little, she couldn't get out often because the lifts didn't work, yet she was grateful and counted her blessings every day. She could have sat there miserable, feeling trapped and helpless, but instead she reframed her thinking and felt truly grateful to be able to see the sun rise over the city. She turned problems into opportunities and never ever felt sorry for herself.

You may be reading this and thinking that the cost of living crisis has left you feeling utterly miserable. That you have had to give up all the lovely treats that made working and living worthwhile – all the things that made you feel nice and that you have come to expect. Miserable is a self-induced mindset. You can think yourself miserable if you feel hard done. You can also think yourself grateful and happy with your lot. Transferring your happiness onto a reliance on external things is a recipe for disaster as it will inevitably come crashing down as fortune changes.

The majority of us love a treat and to feel good about how we look. I feel self-assured and confident when I present my well-groomed self to the world, and have found a way to accept compromises on treats to make me feel great. The pricey monthly manicure has become a set of Primark nails that stay put for two weeks with a good glue, while the fortnightly lash treatment is also a Primark special.

"There is always a thrifty version of your favourite treats available if you roll up your sleeves and look."

The fancy city-centre hairdressers has been traded for an out-of-town salon at half the price, and the once in a while treat of a facial and massage has been swapped for treatments at the local technical college where supervised students offer cost-price beauty treatments. I can still do and have the things that I had before, albeit a shoestring version, and I accept these little compromises which means that I don't feel miserable. There is always a thrifty version of your favourite treats available if you roll up your sleeves and look.

STOICISM

A key belief of the ancient Stoics was the acceptance that we don't react to events, instead we react to our thoughts about them. We can control our thoughts and, therefore, we can control how we respond to any event. They also professed that we should not worry about things that are outside of our control, and that everything in life can be divided into two categories – things that are within our control and things that are not.

I truly believe that a lot of good can come from accepting things that are outside of your control. Getting a grip on what you can and can't control in a challenging situation really is key to finding solutions. By accepting what you can't change, you don't get out your pity pot and sit wallowing in a victim narrative. Identifying the things that you *do* have control over can aid you in identifying opportunities with resilience and flexibility. The diagram below gives a clear indication on what I cannot control and what I *can* control, and therefore where we should put our energy.

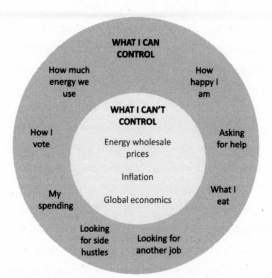

Trying to control the stuff you can't is exhausting and fruitless, and the harsh truth is no one is going to rescue you. Start by taking a long, hard look at what you can do with your current financial

24

situation – what areas do you have influence over or can adapt your lifestyle. Hatch a plan to get through tough times.

My own life has been a higgledy-piggledy path of hard times, better times and then tough times again. I left home and moved to London with 19p in my pocket. I sofa surfed, moved from place to place and blagged my way into jobs that I was ill-qualified to do. I ate a frugal diet and always made sure that I had the underground fare to get to work.

"Trying to control the stuff you can't is exhausting and fruitless, and the harsh truth is no one is going to rescue you."

I bought clothes as I needed them – and for warmth, not vanity. I couldn't control the cost of living in London, all I could control was having somewhere to sleep and earning money to survive. I have lived in rented accommodation where bills were not included, and that meant the heating was never on. I didn't even mither, I just accepted that it was cold for around four months. Maybe that was the folly of youth, but that's how it was – I never once felt sorry for myself. It might have been slightly uncomfortable, but never life-threatening.

After a period of stable work, I bought a home and there was money for holidays and meals out. Then I got pregnant – now there's a life event that knocks you for six financially! I went on to have another child, and out of nowhere my partner was made redundant. Nursery fees (as any parent will know) are insanely expensive, and we qualified for no help. We were living off one modest income.

I couldn't control the cost of nursery fees, I couldn't control the fact that my two young children were unable to fend for themselves; all I could control was our family budget and how we lived. We accounted for every penny and got by: I planned meals, cooked from scratch, bought preloved clothes and entertained the kids with free stuff like parks and outside walks, free or discounted attractions and days out.

As the kids grew older and I progressed on the career ladder at work, we became better off, but still only made financial commitments within our means. Then the cost of living crisis hit, and before we knew it we were feeling the pinch each month. This is when I took stock of our lifestyle again to understand what I could control, and what I could do nothing about. I took control and reframed problems as opportunities.

In the months that it has taken to write this book, I encountered another whopping life change. After 16 years, I separated from my partner. I went from being part of a dual-income household to taking on the two kids, three cats, a mortgage and residual debt from renovation on my own salary and minimum child support. There was a temptation to curl up in a ball and hide, but that's not what I decided to do. Instead, I dusted myself off and recalculated my finances. Shopping at Sainsbury's and Aldi suddenly felt like a luxury, and I researched even cheaper alternatives (Farmfoods for the win!). I accepted that weekly visits to the charity shop for a treat were now out of reach, and I would have to compromise on a monthly chazza shop mooch.

For me, navigating tough financial times is all about keeping a resilient and stoic mindset. Feeling immersed in self-pity makes me feel like a passive victim, and that takes away my control and power in any given situation. I would rather channel that working-class grit and determination, that Brit Blitz spirit, where you dust yourself down, take stock and come up with a new plan for living on your own terms. I appreciate that it is difficult to channel gratitude and resilience during exasperatingly tough times, but for me, feeling negative and sorry for myself makes it nigh on impossible to spot opportunities to be part of my own solution.

LEVELS OF COMFORT

Loads of us Generation Xers like to proclaim, "I grew up in the 1970s, we had single-glazed windows and frost on the net curtains, and we had no heating!" Our standard of living was different; I can remember being cold in bed in winter, but I haven't needed therapy for unresolved childhood trauma because of it. We grew up with three meals a day, no snacks and take outs on birthdays. We only got new outfits for birthdays and Christmas.

Fast-forward 45 years, and as soon as the clocks go back in October the central heating goes on, and we walk around our homes in T-shirts in mid-winter. We step out of cosy homes into cosy cars into cosy workplaces. We have snacks available between meals, and if we fancy a takeaway we just get one because we can't be bothered to cook. We have fast fashion, designed to be worn once and donated, sold or binned; we have fashion micro-seasons. We have access to shopping in the palm of our hand 24/7.

There has to be a middle ground where we consume less, waste less and buy less. The only way to get through harder times is by being able to adjust. It's what our grandparents would call cutting your cloth.

"There has to be a middle ground where we consume less, waste less and buy less."

If you want to spend less and save more something has to give, and really this is down to you. Do you need a fancy £25 face cleanser when Aldi sell cleansers for 99p? Do you need to just click the heating on because it's got a bit colder? The new barometer for heating going on in our house is, "My hands have gone numb and I can't use them any more." In fact, as I haven't used any central heating this year, my tolerance for artificial heat has plummeted and I spent Christmas Day and Boxing Day with the back door and windows open to air the house.

What is the minimum viable standard that you need to be able to function? Do you have to complete a recipe with 12 ingredients or can you improvise and reduce the amount of stuff that you need to buy to make the meal work? Can you plan more affordable tasty, simple meals? Cutting your cloth means taking a long hard look at where you leak money in your spending because you are being aspirational or influenced by marketing, and have become accustomed to a certain level of luxury. Being savvy is about finding that sweet spot where your budget and tolerance levels meet.

One year ago, I was buying that expensive face cleanser, six months ago I was opting for a £10 slightly utilitarian looking cleanser, and now I am as happy throwing a 99p cleanser into my shopping basket – if it does the same thing, I am just as happy; I don't feel deprived and the world didn't stop turning (nor did I break out in boils and pustules).

In short, snobbery and marketing, plus messages about self-care have driven me to waste money on fancy products. Now I can no longer afford them and I am at peace with that. Self-care is not being influenced to buy things outside of my current budget constraints – it's about having the confidence to know that I don't need luxury products to be happy. My new self-care is living within my means and navigating the cost of living crisis on my terms, all the while feeling grateful for what I have and the lessons that I can learn through being skint.

With a mindset of gratitude and acceptance for the things that you can influence or change, you will find that your resilience to deal with tougher financial times is strengthened. You will feel more in control of your budget without self-pity and lack clouding your ability to spot opportunities to hustle and shop savvy. In truth, I love the challenge. I find joy in the things around me that I already have. I enjoy finding clever workarounds to live within my budget and thinking up creative hacks to save even more money where I can. This has not always been my natural mindset; I have had to work at reframing my thinking, but if it can work for me it can work for anyone.

TOP TAKEAWAYS
A THRIFTY MINDSET

- Be really honest with yourself and identify what is a want and what is a need.
- Use the tools in this chapter to become aware of your shopping triggers.
- Practise daily gratitude and acceptance by journaling about people, places and things that make your heart sing with joy. Note down things that have happened during your day that you are grateful for. It is a self-fulfilling prophecy and the more you acknowledge gratitude, the more you will feel content with what you already have.
- Source thriftier versions of self-care treats.
- Remember you cannot control the economy, inflation or the consumer price index. The only things within your control are the income that you generate and the money that you spend. Focus your attention on changing what you can, not what you cannot control.

CHAPTER 2

LIVING BUDGET HEALTH CHECK

Life has more plot twists than a Harlan Coben novel. Life's curveballs, from the minor to the dramatic, impact your budget. So, whether you need to simply take control of your budget or you need to completely re-evaluate, the first step is to really understand how much you are spending and on what, then to take stock and take action where needed.

As the cost of living has risen, I have made changes to my budget incrementally by cutting back in stages. I call this flexing. I started writing this book in December 2022, and by February I had my own major life plot twist: my long-term partner and I separated, leaving me largely responsible for childcare and household costs. I was already living within my means with a modest disposable income and making every single penny count – but I now needed to do more. So, I revisited my budget again. It's important to realise that budget health checks aren't one-offs – this is something that you should systematically revisit when things feel squeezed.

My day job is as a Transformation Project Manager. The majority of what I do involves looking for ways to make changes that result in financial savings. I have applied a lot of the logic and skills that I use within my professional life and adapted them for home. On top of this, in a previous career I managed a government contract that helped vulnerable people manage their debt and budget. These skill sets have stood me in good stead for adopting a system that works on a personal as well as professional level.

The health check has stages which I refer to as **GIFT**, as completing regular health checks can literally save you hundreds of pounds every year.

G – Gather the numbers
I – Insights from the numbers
F – Flex your spending
T – Transform your budget

G: GATHER THE NUMBERS

In simple terms you need to know how much money you have available and how much you are spending. Down to every last penny, it's worth understanding how much life is costing you. This can feel overwhelming, but getting your finances in check is a worthwhile investment of your time. You will need access to your bank statements or online banking, your Amazon account, PayPal, Google Pay, Apple Pay, etc. – basically, anywhere that you make payments from.

INCOME

For most people, income is far easier to calculate than outgoings. In the average household, there are usually far less lines of money coming in than direct debits, standing orders and subscriptions going out.

When calculating the sum total that you have available to spend every month, be sure to take into account:

- salary
- benefits (e.g., child benefit)
- child support
- money from side hustles, etc.

OUTGOINGS

Calculating outgoings can feel like a huge task. There are the standard direct debits that you can read directly from your bank statement, but to really take control of your budget you have to leave no stone unturned. Make sure that you also check the desktop version of PayPal for any regular payments that you may have set up. I discovered a Beauty Club membership that was eating £5 monthly but I couldn't see it on the mobile version of PayPal. Similarly check Google Pay or the App Store for any apps that your darling but sneakily clever kids may have subscribed to without you knowing. These little people are cannier than you may think!

I have included an example health check below, and there is also a blank Health Check available at the back of the book. As you will revisit this process many times, I suggest leaving this blank and copying the table onto your preferred medium – spreadsheet, notebook, etc. There are also specialised apps that you can use for budgeting, but the power is in working through and recording your outgoings with time to pause, reflect and re-evaluate. Remember, when you are hit with a life plot twist you will need to revisit your budget health check and be prepared to flex.

EXAMPLE LIVING BUDGET HEALTH CHECK

Readjusting your budget requires a positive mindset. It's tough to flex down on spending, and it takes being really honest with yourself about what you need and what you want – and this can feel a bit uncomfortable. It's really important to feel gratitude for what you can still afford within your means to stave off any moments of self-pity.

In this example health check, if the costs are fixed, with no wiggle room, I have indicated this with a star in the third column. All other costs are fair game!

In the final column, you'll see a number key that links to information provided in the rest of this chapter – so, for example, if you want to lower your insurance rates, turn to Point 10 in the "F: Flexing your Budget: Ideas and Hacks" section.

The figures in the table are indicative, and the costs after changes are based on some of the changes that I have personally made to dramatically revise my budget.

LIVING BUDGET HEALTH CHECK

What are you spending money on?	Current monthly cost	Costs that can't be changed	Monthly cost after changes	Key to find saving ideas
Rent/ Mortgage	£700		£700	1
Gas/Electric	£230		£140	2
Water	£65		£45	3
Council Tax	£160		£135	4
TV Licence	£13	★	£13	
Secured loans	£100	★	£100	
Debt or loans including student loans, Klarna, etc.	£40	★	£40	
Catalogues	£50		£10	5
Store cards	£30		£10	5
Credit cards	£80		£20	5
Broadband	£50		£30	6
Home telephone	£10		£0	6
TV subscriptions	£30		£0	7
Netflix	£15		£8	8
Spotify	£15		£10	8
Mobile phone contracts	£60		£15	9
Life insurance	£30		£0	10

What are you spending money on?	Current monthly cost	Costs that can't be changed	Monthly cost after changes	Key to find saving ideas
Car insurance	£40		£22	10
Pet insurance	£30		£20	10
Children's trust funds	£60		£20	11
Gym memberships	£80		£40	12
Regular prescriptions	£30		£9	13
Car maintenance	£30	★	£30	
Car fuel	£80		£60	14
Car Tax	£30		£2.50	14
Public transport to school	£120		£120	15
Car parking	£80		£50	16
Clothes & shoes	£100		£50	17
School uniform	£10		£0	17
Pet food	£60		£45	18
Pet medicines & flea treatment	£40		£18	18

LIVING BUDGET HEALTH CHECK

What are you spending money on?	Current monthly cost	Costs that can't be changed	Monthly cost after changes	Key to find saving ideas
Hobbies & clubs	£20		£20	19
Food	£400		£300	20
Cleaning	£20		£15	21
Toiletries	£30		£15	21
Make-up & beauty	£15		£10	21
Hairdressing	£60		£40	22
Amazon Prime	£10		£10	23
Amazon subscriptions	£20		£0	23
Gaming subscriptions, e.g., Xbox Live	£8		£0	24
Google app subscriptions	£6		£0	24
TOTAL	**£3,057**		**£2,173**	

SEEKING PROFESSIONAL HELP

If you do find that your outgoings exceed your monthly income there really is no shame in asking for help. I would recommend speaking to the debt charities StepChange (stepchange.org) or National Debtline (nationaldebtline.org) for information, advice and guidance on contacting people that you may owe money to, advice on what are priority debts and where there may be additional support to help you. Both organisations offer free, impartial services with no agenda.

Becoming a single parent in the middle of a cost of living crisis significantly impacted my budget, and I contacted StepChange for advice before I started budget setting so I could understand what was possible. Mine and my kids' emotional health trumped being financially trapped.

Whatever your situation, there is help available to guide you through life's toughest crossroads and challenges.

I: INSIGHTS FROM THE NUMBERS

Now for the moment of truth! Add up your incomings, add up your outgoings (before any adjustments) and do the maths. What are you left with? Are you left with any wiggle room? Do you have a minus figure? This is where we start to readjust.

F: FLEXING YOUR BUDGET: IDEAS & HACKS

This part of the chapter is a detailed review of everything you purchase on a monthly basis. The purpose of this is to see where you can flex and reduce your outgoings. You can do this incrementally and there are always options within each category to suit your level of comfort.

You do, however, need to do some soul searching and be really honest about what is essential, what is non-essential and what you need to hang on to for fun, entertainment and happiness. This is not about making yourself incredibly miserable and eliminating everything, unless you need or want to.

I'm going to take our example health check and show you how I would work through each non-starred (non-fixed) item on the list (and one starred item!). I am not a financial advisor and have, when needed, taken expert advice. There may be times when you need to speak to an expert, and I will note this in my suggestions.

★ 1. MORTGAGE/RENT

If you have been hit by a temporary bump in the road and are really struggling to pay your mortgage, you may be able to get a mortgage break or move to an interest-only arrangement. Always speak to your provider first to understand what impact this has on your repayments, but it may give you the breathing space you need. If, like me, the change is longer term (I am now paying my mortgage with one income instead of two), it's worth weighing up whether you can downsize and/or move to a different area in your town where house prices are cheaper. It sounds devastating, but this is a reality check – consider whether it is better to compromise and make room in your budget to live, or to hang on to what is essentially just bricks and mortar. You can make anywhere a home, when filled with love.

★ 2. GAS/ELECTRIC

Make sure that you check your usage against payments regularly. With energy prices rising so steeply it's no surprise that the Office of National Statistics reported in February 2023 that 6% of people were in fuel debt. There is lots that you can do to use less energy and reduce your debt (see Chapter 5 – Thrifty Energy Use). You can also negotiate monthly payments with your provider if you offer assurance that you are aiming to reduce consumption. I successfully negotiated 30% off what I was asked to pay by talking my provider through my energy-saving measures.

★ 3. WATER

If you are on a water meter you can reduce your bill by using less. Ways of cutting down water consumption include washing clothes less frequently and limiting showers to 5 minutes (or, even better, showering at the gym if you have a gym membership you don't want to relinquish). These tactics, along with flushing the loo with water collected by my dehumidifier, have reduced my water bill by 25%.

★ 4. COUNCIL TAX

Check to see if you are eligible for any discounts, such as a single person discount. The brilliant website moneysavingexpert.com also has a fabulous step-by-step guide on how to check that your house is in the right Council Tax band. If you have been incorrectly billed at a higher banding you could be eligible for a refund.

★ 5. CATALOGUES, STORE CARDS & CREDIT CARDS

As tempting as it is to buy stuff on credit over a period of time, there is nearly always a catch: either an insane interest rate or inflated initial price. If you have an existing debt that you are struggling to pay, I recommend contacting the catalogue, store card or credit card provider directly and letting them know your situation. You can ask to freeze interest and either pause or recalculate payments. It's always a good idea to get support on how to do this via StepChange or National Debtline, as they have template letters and a list of addresses and numbers that you can use to contact the organisations that you owe money to. Once you have cleared the debt, close the account if you can. If you are paying interest on a credit card, explore options to transfer the balance to a 0% interest card to potentially save yourself hundreds of pounds across the year. Make sure that you close the old account so that you are not tempted to use the card with the empty balance again.

★ 6. BROADBAND & HOME TELEPHONE

Having access to the Internet is as essential as breathing in today's world. We need it to stream TV, kids need it to access online homework, it's essential for work, for play... Need I go on? There are multiple deals and providers out there, so make sure that you are getting the most bang for your buck. It's always worth haggling with your own provider first. I recently contacted

Virgin and reduced my monthly payment by 50% with no lowering of speeds. It's worth the agony of being sat in a call queue to speak with them about reducing your payments. Always mention that you have found a cheaper deal elsewhere (worth researching this using a comparison site first, so that you can back up your claim) and are considering leaving them; if they are stubborn and unrelenting and your contract is up, then take your business elsewhere and transfer to that better deal you found.

It's worth noting that although you don't need an actual phone in your home to get broadband, you *may* require a live phone connection into your home. This is a bit confusing as some providers who use the Openreach network (BT, Sky, TalkTalk, PlusNet, Vodafone, EE) need a line in and others don't. I am with Virgin and there is no need for a phone line, so that cost is eliminated; other providers offer a free landline as part of a broadband package. Make sure you know what you have and what you will need if you are switching. If you don't use your landline, speak to your provider and find out whether you need it and whether you can reduce it to the lowest possible landline package and get a further discount on your bill.

★ 7. TV SUBSCRIPTIONS

Do you really need a gazillion TV channels? How many do you have with your Sky or Virgin package? How many do you actually watch and how many of the channels are total duffs? How many hours of your life have you wasted, mindlessly scrolling menus for something to watch? I completely got rid of my Virgin TV package years ago as the main UK channels are available online for free. I have Netflix and Amazon Prime, and basically the Virgin package was a luxury

I couldn't afford. The kids missed the music channels at first, but you can watch music videos on YouTube for free. If you are serious about scaling back on your budget, bin the pricey TV subscription. I promise you will not miss it as much as you imagine you will!

★ 8. NETFLIX & SPOTIFY

Both of these subscriptions are a luxury that you can either scale back or stop at any time. However, both services offer a choice of subscription plans – such as student, individual, couple and family – so you don't have to abandon them totally. Both of my kids love retreating to their rooms to watch Netflix or listen to music, so they are the things that we have negotiated to keep but we have downgraded our services to save money. Review what you need and adjust your subscription accordingly.

Spotify even offers a free service but it is funded by advertising and you cannot skip through tracks – but, hey ho, it's free, and when push comes to shove you are here to save money.

Netflix offers different plans depending on how many devices will be streaming at one time. Take the opportunity to review how you watch TV: if you have younger children that do not watch much TV unsupervised, or you can get the family into one room to watch TV together, you can downgrade to the cheapest Basic plan. You will also save energy watching TV in one room.

★ 9. MOBILE PHONES

I can remember wishing my mobile phone contract period away so that I could upgrade to the latest snazziest handset. I would open the box with my new phone in to quickly realise it did all the same stuff that my old phone did: made calls, connected to the Internet and took photos; it just looked a bit fresher and prettier and the battery was in its prime. What a fool I was, drawn in by marketing.

I have now had my current phone for four years. Once the initial contract was up, I opted not to upgrade and get a new contract, and set up a way cheaper SIM only deal using my existing handset. I saved myself £60 a month instantly by keeping my old handset. The battery may not be at its optimum, but I work from home most of the time, and even when I am in an office I can always pop the phone on charge when I get there.

My children get refurbished handsets bought online from a reputable online reseller (try Back Market, backmarket.co.uk) and a SIM only deal. Getting a contract phone for a kid is a recipe for disaster, as they will lose, decimate or go swimming with a phone in their pocket (true story!) – it is highly likely that the contract and financial burden will outlive your child's handset.

★ 10. INSURANCE POLICIES

Nowadays, most of us all well versed in price comparison websites and in shopping around for insurance. Nevertheless, sometimes it's easier to let it slide and simply renew because you can't be bothered to switch provider. It really isn't a faff, and switching could save you hundreds a year if you use Compare the Market (comparethemarket.com), Go Compare (gocompare.com) or even some of the direct insurance websites such as Direct Line (directline.com) to get quotes.

There is also the question of whether you need insurance. For example, if you claim some means-tested benefits you may qualify for PDSA Vet treatment for your pet rather than pay a premium. I am not suggesting that you cancel your pet insurance, but do check whether you would qualify for free emergency help. If you have death in service life cover with your job, can you really afford an additional life insurance premium?

As I mentioned earlier, I am not a financial advisor so do consult an expert to understand the impact of making changes to any of your insurance policies. I am sharing hacks and tips to save money and both pet and life insurances are a luxury if you can get the same cover for free elsewhere.

★ 11. CHILDREN'S TRUST FUNDS

As a working-class kid, the notion of trust funds was alien to me – trust funds were for the well-heeled kids from the posh end of town. However, UK children born between 2002 and 2011 qualified for a free starting payment voucher to encourage all parents, regardless of wealth and income, to start a trust fund. You had a choice to either just sit on the initial investment or top it up with monthly or occasional payments. If you add in monthly and it's become unaffordable, consider reviewing, lowering or ceasing payments. You may wish to seek advice from a financial advisor as there may be alternative options, but if we are talking about lowering expenditure then this saving pot is very much a "nice to have" rather than an essential.

★ 12. GYM MEMBERSHIPS

A gym membership *is* a luxury, *but* exercise is important for physical and mental health. I do think it's worth weighing up the preventative health benefits of your gym membership before completely abandoning it. Mine pays for itself as I shower, dry my hair and charge my phone there.

And not all gyms are made the same. There are luxury gyms with spa-like facilities, top of the range equipment and all the latest fitness craze classes, where the "guests" wear top-of-the-range sports gear and smell divine. Then there are spit and sawdust community gyms and budget, barely manned, 24-hour gyms. It's not actually the surroundings that get you fit and healthy and looking buff, it's your commitment, consistency and effort.

If you joined the gym in January and have used it twice, maybe it's not for you. If you are a member of a no-contract gym, just cancel your membership; if you are committed to a contract and cannot leave, then downgrade to the lowest package until your contract is up.

Consider changing your swanky gym for one of the chain gyms, such as Pure Gym or The Gym Group, where membership can work out at around just £5 a week, and if you shower there daily it literally pays for itself by the end of the month with what you have saved on water and energy.

If you are really strapped for cash, Facebook Marketplace is awash with exercise equipment resulting from other people's failed New Year and lockdown resolutions. If you have space in your budget for the cost of one month's gym membership, can you create an exercise space in your home and save on membership completely?

★ 13. REGULAR PRESCRIPTIONS

A few years back I woke with my back in absolute spasm – I couldn't move. I was trapped on my bed, lying on my side, and I had to wee in a cup! Luckily, I could speak between stabbing pains and groaning and the GP wrote an emergency prescription. Little did I know at the time that I would require three separate prescription items each month for the next 12 months? At over £9 a pop that's one pricey back injury. My saviour was my local pharmacist who told me about the annual prescription prepayment certificate (PPC). Currently £111.60 for a year (or £31.25 for 3 months), the savings are immediate as you can pay in 10 monthly instalments by direct debit. If you don't qualify for free prescriptions and are managing a health condition with prescription medicine, it's an absolute must. As a healthy person who avoids going to the doctor like the plague, I had no exposure to the world of long-term illness, so this little gem saved me a fortune. You can apply on the NHS website – just Google "buy a prescription prepayment certificate" and it will pop up. How's my back? After medicine, physio and a chiropractor failed to deliver, I fixed it myself by strengthening my glutes and hamstrings at the gym (posterior chain!) – this is why I swear that the gym membership is essential.

HEIDI'S HINTS
HRT HELP

For women experiencing menopause symptoms who have been prescribed hormone replacement therapy (HRT), there is a specific HRT PPC available for just £19.30 for 12 months.

★ 14. CAR STUFF: REPAYMENTS, TAX AND FUEL

As in many of these sections, when it comes to your car there is a sliding scale of options, depending on how much you need to flex down. The ultimate questions in relation to car expenses are:

- Do you need a car, or do you want a car?
- What do you use it for – how many essential trips do you make?
- Could you walk or take public transport?
- If you are a two-car household, could you share a vehicle?
- Are you rural or semi-rural with poor public transport? It's a tricky one as giving up the comfort of going from a warm(ish!) house to a toasty car on a cold morning holds way more appeal than standing at a bus stop with rain lashing down, vertically and sideways, only to be met with a cancelled route.

If you are wedded to having a car, there are still saving options to consider.

Do you need the car you have, i.e., is it flashy and on finance or lease? Is it fur coat and no knickers? Are you driving around in a flashy motor and eating beans on toast every day? Is it worth being that skint to drive something to impress other people? Like with most of my suggestions, buy used, preloved, preowned, whatever you want to call it.

Consider downsizing your car to one that has the lowest possible annual tax, efficient fuel consumption, is cheap to insure and is known to be a reliable model. Or try and find a used car with low mileage that is a refurbished insurance write-off. If you are driving an old banger anyway, look into whether you could switch to third party insurance instead of fully comprehensive?

The point here is the difference between what you want and what you need, and requires some serious soul searching. Be honest with yourself about what is about ego, image and want, and what is about getting from A to B.

★ 15. PUBLIC TRANSPORT

It's an obvious question, but one that you need to ask is: Could you walk this?

If the answer is yes, on a dry day, do that, and save the cost of the bus or tube ticket for when it's hammering it down. If you can walk, turn it into a positive and invest in a step monitor, such as a Fitbit. You could rack up steps, getting in free cardio in the fresh air – walking is well-proven to be good for your mind and body.

If the journey is unwalkable, is there a season ticket, pass or concession that you could buy? Or could you work from home part of the week?

If you pay for public transport for your children, how far is it to walk, and do they have friends that walk? Would they consider walking on dry days? Kids are a bit more cosseted now than when I was growing up, but a short walk to school is cheaper and better for their fitness if they can walk safely in a small group.

★ 16. CAR PARKING

Again, it's an obvious one; could you walk instead? If not, it's worth noting that, depending on your Local Authority, not all car parks charge the same. In the city where I live, a large, well-lit city centre car park costs £1 more per hour or £100 more for a monthly pass than a slightly out of town (6-minute walk) car park where you can purchase a monthly unlimited pass for £50. It really is worth the 6-minute stroll if you are parking daily. Visit your local authority's parking pages and review car parks to find out which is the cheapest option for you; and if you park daily for work, investigate whether a monthly season ticket is more affordable, if available.

★ 17. CLOTHES, SHOES & SCHOOL UNIFORM

I have written a whole chapter on buying preloved clothes (Chapter 8, Look Stylish For Less), but the pertinent questions when making a new clothing purchase are: Could you wear or restyle something from your existing wardrobe? Do you *really need* something new or do you *want* something new? Could you borrow from a friend to scratch the itch of needing something new?

School uniform *has* to be bought as those darn kids grow, and then they grow some more. My son went from a size 7 shoe to a size 11 in four months. The struggle is real and chuffing expensive. I always sell on outgrown blazers and PE kits in Facebook Marketplace and reuse the money to rebuy one in a bigger size, either off Marketplace or from our local school uniform reuse shop (this runs on donations); it is also worth checking the Olio app under the non-food section for uniform. If there seems to be none available, you could put out a "want" post on Marketplace or Olio as someone might just be ready to offload some outgrown items. Preloved white shirts can be washed in bleach, nothing fancy, just wallop some normal thick bleach in the washing machine tray and it brings them up sparkling new.

It is the logoed blazers and PE kits that cost a mint, and if you can find these preloved you will save a small fortune. Of course, there is the option to buy these a size bigger and adopt that old-school mum mantra of "You will grow into it", while your little cherubs pootle off to school with sleeves trailing alongside their calves and a gap round the neck you could fly a plane through.

★ 18. PETS

The cost of everything has risen dramatically, and that includes pet food, pet medicine and flea treatments.

Could you shop around and buy in bulk to get economy of scale? I buy large boxes of pet food on Amazon; the delivery is free and I get 16 packs extra per box than if I purchased from a high street pet store. It is even cheaper on Amazon's "subscribe and save" option. If your pet gets the top of the range, crème de la crème meat and kibble, could you switch for a slightly cheaper brand? It's an emotive subject because pets are our fur children and very often they can be cuddlier, more well-mannered and more loving than our skin children (can you tell I have teens?). You also can't reason with animals to explain that they won't be getting their favourite meal. That said, would an animal let itself starve out of pure stubbornness? I'm not so sure.

My cats love Dreamies – they are like cat crack. The Aldi version of these were a third of the branded cost, so I gave the cats a pack a day between them. But now they've more than doubled in price (what the actual fudge!), so I have stopped with the treats and switched for plain old boring kibble. Guess what the cats did... they ate the cheap stuff.

With medicines and flea treatments it may be cheaper to ask the vet for a prescription, rather than purchase medicine from the surgery; there are many online vets that sell treatments cheaper that just require a prescription. The same goes for flea treatments: look at the cost of Indorex in your vets compared to Amazon and there is my case in point; my vet recently added a massive £7 mark up on one can.

Check the active ingredient in your flea or worm treatment and google to see if you can find a cheaper version. The treatment I was buying cost £60 per month, for my three cats. I get the equivalent treatment for £18 online. The key takeaway here (as elsewhere) is to shop around.

★ 19. HOBBIES & CLUBS

Hobbies and interests, groups and clubs make up the fabric of our lives and add to our multi-faceted identities; they give us social connections and a community of interest that is good for our emotional wellbeing. There are free clubs and activities, of course, but there are also groups that attract a subscription fee. Paying a fee is all well and good if you use it, but if you have any sort of membership that you have let lapse, just cancel it – if you haven't accessed it in three months you are wasting money.

★ 20. FOOD

There is a whole chapter on food (Chapter 6, Money-saving Grocery Shopping). The big issue for me here is that it is important to drop any preconceptions or assumptions about supermarket pricing. The landscape has changed since the cost of living crisis hit and it pays to shop around. On the flip side, drop any snobbery about budget shops like Farmfoods and Iceland – frozen vegetables and meat are a lot cheaper than fresh, and for me, personally, there is less waste from frozen veg as you get a number of servings without it turning into a fetid mess in the fridge drawer.

★ 21. CLEANING, TOILETRIES, MAKE-UP & BEAUTY

I have bundled these unlikely bedfellows together as the message is very similar: steer away from pricey brands. If you are serious about saving money, ask yourself whether you need the branded fabric softener, branded facewash, high-end bronzer, fancy shampoo and exorbitant face cream?

The quickest and easiest way to save money on these products is to drop the label snobbery. If you buy into the beauty claims that the manufacturers make, you need to give your head a wobble. Moisturisers, serums, potions and lotions temporarily hydrate and plump the skin, but there isn't a magic cream that reverses ageing. I am not a doctor or a dermatologist, but common sense tells me you can't banish wrinkles with a £200 cream (Botox maybe, cream no). Whatever branded stuff you are buying, there will be an Aldi dupe somewhere in store that will do the job. If you are cutting your cloth, you can't afford to be misguidedly snobby about branded and high-end products. It's way more fun finding a cheaper version of a posh thing and boasting about that than being one of the suckers that is pulled in by advertising and editorial claims. We have been conditioned to covet fancy stuff in the name of self-care and self-love, but does it really make us happier, thinner, less wrinkled or more joyful?

★ 22. HAIRDRESSING

Remember the heady days of the COVID-19 pandemic lockdown? Lockdown hair led to salons being booked up for months in advance when the world opened up again. Left completely rogue, dishevelled hair can make us look like an understudy for Tom Hanks in *Castaway*; and if you are in face-to-face meetings, greeting customers or on a Teams call, an unruly mop doesn't translate very well into the world of (most) work.

There is, however, a sliding scale of options available to save you money in hairdressing, listed here from high to low cost.

- **Top-end,** city-centre hairdressers where you are greeted with a glass of bubbly and canapés. Rents and business rates are highest in city centres and those bottles of bubbly aren't really free – you will be paying way more than you need to.
- **Out of town**, smaller hairdressers will be much cheaper. There is one technical college in our city and 90% of the local hairdressers have been there and done the same training; there are two hairdressing supplies warehouses, so they all use more or less the same products; and their rents and business rates are cheaper. This all adds up to a very similar service, for at least 30% cheaper than that city-centre salon.
- **Mobile hairdressers** have no premises to pay for and this saving is passed onto you, plus they come to your house – it's a win-win.
- **Trainees and juniors**: does your local technical college offer hairdressing sessions at a hugely discounted rate? The hair cut may take longer when you let a student loose on your hair but you literally just pay for the products and all work is supervised. Similarly, if there is a trainee in your local salon it may cost less to use them.

- **DIY** is always an option if cash is really tight. Box colour formulations *are* better nowadays than they used to be (but nothing beats the colours that the hairdresser uses, especially if you are trying to lighten your hair). For every ten blonde box dyes sold there must be at least two tales of woe, resulting in an expensive correction at the hairdressers and a matted fuzz of candyfloss breakage. Risk at your peril. Whenever I have attempted to lighten my own hair I have visited one of the hairdressing suppliers and bought salon-grade products to use at home; it's cheaper than a salon visit but at least you know that you will (hopefully) get the desired result. It's not so risky going darker with a box dye, but I personally wouldn't risk it with a blonde.

When it comes to a haircut, however, I have never been brave enough to take more than a snip off the front of my own hair; but clippers for short hair are a great option to save a fortune.

★ 23. AMAZON

I have added Amazon as so many of us subscribe to Amazon Prime and continue to do so without really thinking about it. Do you use the TV Streaming, Amazon Music and order a number of items monthly? If the answer is yes then it's probably worth it. If you don't watch any of the TV shows, listen to Amazon Music and order one item a month then it is worth weighing up whether it's cheaper to buy the item elsewhere and pay postage.

I probably shouldn't admit to this but, on occasion, I have ordered something on Amazon Subscribe and Save to get the discount, then to my surprise I have received it again the next month! If you do scour for discounts *always* cancel the subscription once you have received the item (unless you want or need recurring deliveries that is). If you do opt for a recurring delivery, check the price prior to dispatch as they do fluctuate and your one-time bargain may not be such a steal.

★ 24. GAMING & GOOGLE APP SUBSCRIPTIONS

If you (like me) are guilty of keeping kids occupied and meltdowns at bay by offering up your phone in the doctor's waiting room, or in long queues and on boring journeys, do a regular check on your Google or App Store subscriptions. It's so easy for kids to buy in-app purchases and upgrade to a premium version if your card is connected – and, hey presto, you are subscribed to some bizarre ad-free version of a game for a year. I can hear you saying, "Tell them not to click on any extras"; yes, there is that, but as extra precaution do a regular check to make sure you are not paying for any apps. The same goes for live console games where they can make in-game purchases.

T: TRANSFORM YOUR BUDGET

Once you have gathered all the information relating to where you spend money and have found opportunities to flex, you can work through the figures replacing them with the thriftier options to transform your budget.

The example Living Budget Health Check shows a whopping £884 of savings that can be made. As I mentioned earlier, it is based on changes that I personally made – some of them painless, others a little more drastic (such as swapping the car for a far less fuel-hungry beast with really low annual tax, and relinquishing the use of central heating all winter).

TOP TAKEAWAYS
LIVING BUDGET HEALTH CHECK

Apply the same principles whatever the expense:

- Can you do without it?
- Can you find the same thing cheaper?
- Can you flex down on the service or product? Set yourself measurable goals and try one or two of the hacks on for size. How much did you save? How did this make you feel?
- Revisit your heath check at least every six months to see where you can flex.
- Remember you are not denying yourself by taking a more economical option, you are being savvy, canny and winning at life,
- Being thrifty is a **GIFT.**

CHAPTER 3

THRIFTY HABITS & STRATEGIES

It is so easy to get trapped in habits, financial and otherwise, that no longer serve us. I am no pious finance wizard; I am just a bog-standard imperfect human with poor impulse control and excruciating self-awareness. Although what suits us at one stage of our lives may not continue to fit as we meander down life's wonky and unpredictable path, the trouble with habits is that – once you are in a groove – autopilot kicks in. It requires a conscious decision and self-discipline to re-route to get into new, healthier habits and ways of thinking about anything, including money and spending.

I have created a series of habit restarts that help me to control spending when willpower alone isn't cutting it. Be aware though, if you attempt to make all of these changes at once it might feel a bit overwhelming; you will be setting yourself up to fail. Go gently on yourself – set a goal of changing one or two spending habits at a time. See how it feels, try it on for size, set yourself an achievable goal. This is a pick and mix of hacks that you can use to help you to spend less.

Despite popular opinion that you can assign a set number of days to forming a new habit, *Psychology Today* reports that there are too many unknown variables in individual circumstances to scientifically apply a target timescale to forming new habits. Changed behaviour has a much greater chance of sticking if it yields rewards, i.e. you get a dopamine hit, a buzz and a feeling of satisfaction or pleasure from your changed behaviour. It is therefore really important to reframe your thinking and identify what will make you feel great about spending and wasting less money.

As you set yourself a goal to change a habit it is a really good idea to build in some tangible measures to review your progress. This will allow you to see where you're making positive changes so that you can feel the reward. For me, seizing opportunities to save money is as dopamine-inducing as payday splurging – and much healthier for my bank balance. Throughout this chapter, I will show you money-saving opportunities, from which you will create positive habit changes. Look out for "Heidi's Hints" through the book.

HEIDI'S HINTS
MEASURE THE CHANGE

If you have a tendency to splurge after payday, one of the most useful things you can do in measuring your progress is to **find your baseline**. Do this by noting down how many days of the month you are cash-strapped and scrabbling around for pocket change. Look at your online banking: Is there a huge glut of transactions in the first week, then tumbleweed and direct debits for the remainder of the month?

PAYDAY MILLIONAIRE SYNDROME

Hands up if you get paid monthly! Do you have a mental shopping list that you have been fantasising about since a week after you were last paid? Do you splurge on payday, "because you deserve it"? Roll on one, maybe two weeks after payday and you are struggling to fathom how you will make it through the rest of the month. You feel hard done by, like you are on a pointless hamster wheel of working for nothing and wishing the month away until next payday. Don't worry, you are not alone. The online platform *Finance Digest* reported that 43% of Brits spend nearly half of their disposable income within 24 hours of being paid; an astounding 81% is spent within seven days of being paid.

We all like to enjoy life and treat ourselves, and that healthy payday online balance – not yet sullied by direct debits, bills and standing orders – can lull you into a false sense of security; it can make you feel richer than you are and the spendy payday millionaire cycle begins. Here are my top tips for breaking this cycle.

CALCULATE YOUR DISPOSABLE INCOME

In Chapter 2 you completed the Living Budget Health Check. From this, you can calculate the amount that is your disposable income: it is the money you have left after all your essential outgoings (regular bills) to spend on treats, days out, rainy day emergencies. To calculate your daily disposable income, divide this leftover sum by the number of days in the month. So, if you have £300 left after all the bills and food are paid for you have £10 a day in a 30-day month. It's not as much as you thought, is it? Carry the reality of this figure in your head at all times. Value every single £1 that you spend.

"Value every single £1 that you spend."

Completing this exercise is a good reality check, as it will put that £50 ad hoc spend you made in B&M Stores into perspective when you work out that it is actually over 16% of your monthly disposable income.

THE HAPPINESS SCALE

Complete the following exercise *after* payday. Make a copy of the blank Happiness Scale table available at the back of this book, or find something else to write or make a record on – a piece of paper, a journal, a spending diary, spreadsheet, etc. – and note down what you bought last month between **Day 1 and Day 14 after payday**. Use your online banking or bank statement to help you to remember what you spent and where you shopped. **Do not include regular bills and outgoings** – you are creating a list of the additional purchases you made.

Now, on a scale of 1–5, jot down how amazing that item has made you feel over the past two to four weeks since you purchased it. If it was a perceived essential purchase, use the scale to measure and record how useful it has been in the last month. See the example below.

The Happiness Scale

Item	Cost	Type of purchase	Scale of 1–5 Happiness/ Usefulness	Reason for score
School shoes	£35	Essential	5	Wears them every day and are mandatory
Charity shop blue velvet suit	£12	Non-essential	1	It's been a month and I haven't worn it; it was an impulse buy
Brunch with best friend	£9	Non-essential	5	Time with my bestie is like a therapy session and I felt great after
Bronzer from Primark	£4	Non-essential	1	There were no testers and it's the wrong shade
Sequin top from charity shop	£3	Non-essential	2	I really like it, but I haven't worn it; and I'm a magpie for sequins
Two candles from Aldi	£8	Non-essential	3	Nice while they lasted – they made me feel warm and cosy for a few hours

You can see from my list there is over £25 worth of stuff that isn't really bringing me any happiness or proving useful a month after buying it.

This exercise takes some soul searching, but doing this helps you to really stop, analyse and challenge yourself on past purchases and impulse buys. It helps you to see the futility of many of your spends, and makes you stop and think about how much money you have wasted on payday millionaire treats. This, in combination with the Seven-Step Self-Evaluation exercise found in Chapter 1, is a powerful tool to tackle payday millionaire spending.

A lunch out with a friend you haven't seen for ages that lifts your spirits for weeks is priceless, as is a day out with the kids – making memories that you will remember for years is priceless. As for clothes or bits and bobs you don't actually *need*, if they don't bring joy a month after you've purchased them... well, why buy them in the first place? Getting into the habit of reviewing your spending is a good way of becoming more conscious of your habits.

HEIDI'S HINTS
MEASURE THE CHANGE

- Use the Happiness Scale table to discover how much you could have saved on purchases that are neither useful nor bringing you ongoing happiness.
- My example above, based on actual purchases, shows I spent £25 on impulse buys in just two weeks.

THE 21-DAY HABIT

Now here is a revelation for the payday millionaire – you don't have to spend every last penny of your disposable income every month. Start the month by writing a list of the things (and their cost) that you *need* to buy and the things that you would *like* to buy. How much do they add up to? Does the total exceed your disposable income? How would you feel if, for once, you ended the month with cash for a rainy day or extra funds toward something spectacular? How would you feel if you weren't surviving on budget ramen noodles by the middle of the month?

> **"You don't have to spend every last penny of your disposable income every month."**

Could you go 21 days without buying "stuff"? By adopting the "one day at a time" principle that they use in Alcoholics Anonymous, can you get through a single day without spending? If you set yourself an immediate goal of 21 days it may feel unsurmountable – instead, try taking it one day at a time. It is far easier to resist temptation over a 24-hour period than it is over multiple weeks. Not buying anything "just for today" is achievable, and once you have got through one day, you can apply the principle to the next day and keep going. Repeat the mantra, "Just for today I will not make any unnecessary purchases," morning, noon and night to keep reminding yourself of your commitment on a daily basis. This principle will help you to achieve spendy abstinence by breaking it into more manageable chunks. You can do anything for just one day.

Most payday millionaires don't buy anything for 21 days anyway, but it's an enforced 21-day no spend period as they have burned through all of their pennies after seven days and spend the rest of the month in purgatory, dreaming of what they will buy when their bank account is topped up. What would it feel like if you *reversed* this? What if you couldn't start buying things that you wanted or needed until 21 days *after* payday? This gives you a great cooling-off period that should help prevent you frittering cash on useless purchases that won't bring you ongoing joy. It will also mean that you won't feel miserable as you deplete all your spends within a week and start to chip into your grocery budget.

Waiting 21 days to start spending helps to dissociate payday from splurging. And, most of all, you are not staring at an empty bank account for the majority of the month. If you only have a week's window before next payday, only one weekend to hit the shops (unless you take a week off work and go into a buying frenzy), you should be able to roll some of your disposable income over into the next month. This will help you to gain some discipline and slow down on spending, and even start saving.

To make this work you do need to be mindful of not making shopping destinations a leisure activity on days out, and you do need to avoid online shops. The steps below will make the 21-day habit easier to stick to and after a few months, when you feel how much more control you have gained, you will want to stick at it.

Exercise: The 21-day habit

- Calculate your monthly and daily disposable income.
- Write a list of the things that you NEED to buy and a list of the things that you WANT to buy.
- Review the Need list. Are they *all* essential? Move them to the Want list if you are fibbing to yourself.
- Go ahead and buy the essential things that you need. For example, I needed to buy new school shoes for my son as the sole fell off one of his. (It only took him a week to realise he had been walking around with one soleless shoe!)
- Recalculate your monthly and daily disposable income after you have purchased your essential items.
- Set the date – 21 days after payday – when you can buy the things you want.
- Take your card details off your phone and also off Google Pay or Apple Pay.
- Temporarily delete eBay, Vinted and other shopping apps from your phone.
- Tell a close friend what you are doing and ask them to be your mentor for when you feel the itch to spend before 21 days. If your resolve starts to weaken, talk to them, offload your pain, and ask them to challenge and support you. Give your debit card to your friend to look after so you have to ask for it. It's a great idea to do this challenge together for mutual support, but be mindful of enabling each other to fall back into spendy habits too.
- One day at a time. Repeat the mantra: "*Just for today I will not buy things that I do not absolutely need.*" If you feel the urge to impulse buy, remember to repeat the mantra

and distract yourself. Put your phone away, go for a walk, meditate, go for a workout, call your mentor buddy. It will pass.

- Make plans at the weekend or on days off where shopping isn't the activity: catch up with friends for a walk or coffee; attend a gym class; watch a movie or your favourite show; have a pamper session. Just do anything that *isn't* shopping.
- Day 21: review your Want list. How many of those things don't feel as important now you have had time to cool off?
- Day 21: go shopping for some of the things that you want (if there are still any you want that is!).

HEIDI'S HINTS
MEASURE THE CHANGE

- On your first month of practising the 21-day habit, make a note of how much money you have left on payday. How does that make you feel?
- Are you able to transfer any money into a saving pot? How does that make you feel?

DIGITAL CASH STUFFING

There is plenty of advice, books and guides on cash stuffing out there. This is the principle where you draw cash out of your bank and allocate it to your outgoings in separate, labelled plastic wallets, taking only the cash you need to help you to stay within a budget. Now, whatever you think of the demise of cash, it's a reality: if you do your grocery shop online because you can't get to the store in person, or if you use the self-scan handsets at the supermarket, or simply because a retailer doesn't take cash, you will soon realise you are pretty stuffed if you have withdrawn cash and popped it into envelopes. As the world becomes increasingly digital, we need to modernise the principle by turning it into digital cash stuffing.

There are lots of free, online-only digital banks that let you open an account with a few clicks online and issue a card. The important bit is that many of them allow you to create different pots or "saving spaces" for different categories of spending. Most only let you spend from the main pot/space, so there is a physical action required to transfer money from one pot to another before you make a purchase. This is good because, if you are an impulse shopper, it's an extra step to slow you down. It gives you the opportunity to ask yourself whether you really need it, a moment to reflect and decide whether to buy or put the item back from whence it came. These cards also allow you to make free cash withdrawals from the hole in the wall if needed, and may offer cashback and interest.

THE ACCOUNTS/POTS THAT I USE ARE:

Current account

- Direct debits and standing orders, including mortgage, utilities, Council Tax, etc.
- Groceries
- Petrol and car costs
- Pets

Disposable income account
- Pocket Money – for essential and non-essential items
- Christmas and Birthdays – savings pot
- The Fun Pot – savings pot for days out and events

Savings account
- Winter fuel – savings pot (this is in a separate interest-paying savings account; I only pay my energy provider what I use, not more, as the money is better off in my bank account gathering 3.4% interest)

HOW TO GET STARTED

Once you have completed your Budget Health Check in Chapter 2, you will know EXACTLY how much you need in your current account for regular bills and how much you have allocated for groceries, petrol, pets, etc., and what disposable income you have left. Choose a current account that pays cashback on all purchases, as groceries and car costs are often the biggest expenditures each month. Bills are paid from your main account and purchases are made using your cashback account.

Transfer the rest of your money (after bills) into your cashback account and organise it into pots. I always keep my Pocket Money pot empty and store this money in the savings pot. Doing this means that I have to log into my account and transfer money between pots before I make a purchase. This slows me down further; it makes me think again, do I really need this?

When you go out and you do not intend to buy anything, do NOT take your debit card for your disposable income account with you. Leave it with a trusted friend, remove your debit card from your phone so you cannot use this to pay. This is a sure-fire way to avoid those "accidental" spur-of-the-moment purchases.

THE 8-DAY GROCERY WEEK

For as long as I can remember we have done a weekly food shop. The day before shopping day, the fridge looks bare, there are no obvious goodies to grab and the kids are generally grumbling that there is nothing to eat. At first glance, it does indeed look like there is nothing to eat, but as the cost of food has gone up, and up and up again, I thought I'd try something new. What if, on Day 7, we didn't go shopping? What if we had an "iffits" dinner.

An "iffits" dinner is basically: if it's in the cupboard, freezer or fridge, that's what we are eating. While green beans, chicken nuggets and macaroni cheese is not going to win *MasterChef*, it will fill hungry bellies and provides protein, veg and carbs. It's surprising how much extra you can drag out of a weekly shop by getting creative with the dregs of the fridge and freezer. I've started using AI technology, such as ChatGTP, to help make sense of my leftovers: I list the ingredients and ask it what I can cook with the food that I have scavenged. This saves me time (as well as money) as the AI tool does the heavy lifting and scours the Internet to find recipes for me. I would recommend getting a few cartons of long-life milk and freezing a loaf if you are doing this to make sure you don't cave and shop early for essentials.

> **"It's surprising how much extra you can drag out of a weekly shop by getting creative with the dregs of the fridge and freezer."**

71

If you spend £70 a week on groceries, that's £10 a day. By adopting the 8-day grocery week and eking out the dregs of the fridge, freezer and cupboards, you could save £40 a month or £520 over a year. Another added benefit is that it reduces food waste as you use up the random and rogue items lurking in the bottom of the freezer instead of binning them. (I swear I cannot even remember buying halloumi burgers and packet curried lentils.)

HEIDI'S HINTS
MEASURE THE CHANGE

- How much does your food shop cost when you work it out as a daily figure?
- How much could you save if you dragged the previous week's grocery shopping out an extra day before topping up?
- Use AI technology such as ChatGTP to help you rustle up meals from leftovers.

THE MONDAY TO WEDNESDAY RULE

If you don't quite have the mettle for the 21-day habit, the Monday to Wednesday Rule is another great way of tempering spending. It doesn't have to be specifically Monday to Wednesday, pick any three days in the week that suit you... and don't buy a single thing for those three days. Nada, nish, nothing. Do not step foot in a shop, don't browse online stores, do not add stuff to virtual baskets. And don't even buy a coffee, packed lunch, newspaper, magazine. Nothing at all.

Even if you have been to the supermarket armed with a shopping list, there is always something you forget that feels essential, or something else you feel you need. Unless it's life or death, don't top up. What would happen if you have to go three days without it?

I started to practise this rule as I am awful at going into the supermarket for one or two emergency items and spotting a yellow sticker item, an introductory offer or BOGOF deal and spending more than I intended.

I have always been a sucker for a discount store: B&M, The Range, Poundland, Home Bargains. I would pop out for a mooch – I had developed a habit of using "discount" shopping as a boredom buster – or I would go in for one specific item and always return with at least £20 worth of non-essential bits and bobs. Those extra bits soon add up if you repeat the habit a few times a month. The three-day no spend rule helped me to temper this habit and superfluous spending.

HEIDI'S HINTS
MEASURE THE CHANGE

- How much do you spend in the few days after grocery shopping? Do you top up with extras during the week?
- Do you buy something most days? How much could you save if you allocated no spend days?

CLOTHES SHOPPING DETOX

I made a New Year's resolution that I would not buy any clothes until after March. Even though I already only bought preloved fashion from charity shops, Vinted and car boot sales, it still adds up. I looked through my bank account and I was easily spending at least £20 a week on preloved clothes. If I am truly honest with myself, I do not NEED any more clothes. Sure, I like the novelty of new, I like shiny things, and I love rummaging through charity shops – but I absolutely do not NEED another item of clothing, the soles are not falling off my shoes, the clothes I have are not falling apart, and the clothes I have suit the season we are in.

I managed 10 weeks out of 12. I fell just short of my goal of three months due to a hideous relationship breakdown. This taught me a major life lesson: when times get tough, I get shopping. I told you, I am not a perfect, virtuous human – which is exactly why I have developed these strategies.

However, when I did go out shopping after ten weeks of abstinence, I was way more cautious and conscious. Previously, I could easily have come out of a charity shop with five or six items to show off on an Instagram haul. The shopping detox worked wonders, as I bought a mere two items and even then felt a bit guilty. My purchases were way more considered. I haven't gone back to my old habits of feeling like I needed to buy something every week, and I have broken the habit of buying way more than I need.

HEIDI'S HINTS
MEASURE THE CHANGE

- How much do you spend per week or per month on clothes?
- How much could you save if you did a three-month clothes shopping detox? I personally saved £200, which I used for my car MOT.

CLEANSE, PURGE & RAISE SOME FUNDS

Organizing guru Marie Kondo has made a mint from persuading people to chuck stuff out, so I am not going to go into lots of detail about things "sparking joy". This is *my* super simple system for decluttering to make some cash.

CLOTHES

If it's coming to the end of winter and you haven't worn a particular coat, jumper, pair of boots or other wintery bits all season, get rid. If it's the end of summer and you haven't worn a summer item all season, again, get rid.

Dead simple.

I do, however, have a purgatory rail. This is for things that I know I haven't worn, won't wear and should get rid of, but for some bizarre reason feel an emotional attachment to. These clothes usually involve sequins, gold lamé or sparkle; and for a lady in her mid-50s who doesn't go anywhere more exciting than the supermarket, they have no real place in my wardrobe. I let things fester on the rail for a month. If they remain unworn after the month, guess what? I get rid. You have to be brutal, but the purgatory rail helps to protect against seller's remorse, which is a painful condition that arises when you get caught up in the moment of making a few quid and let something really special go to a new home. I did this with a 1992 Vivienne Westwood corset that I sold for £30 in 2006 – and is now valued at £1,300.

Repeat the clothes purge every six months.

My top tips for selling clothes

- Some clothes have zero hanger appeal, particularly black dresses. For these items, it helps if you can show what the item looks like on. Take a picture of you wearing it; you can use your photo editor on your phone to scribble out your face if you are feeling coy.

- If you are using Royal Mail postage it is cheaper to post a large letter than it is a small parcel. So, if you can get a blouse or smaller item into a C5 size envelope, or if you can fold a parcel bag in half and tape it down it will cost less to post. It also has to be letterbox width. Post offices have sample letter boxes that you can push your postage item through to check if it's a letter or a parcel. Always ask the staff to wiggle it a bit to get it through to qualify for the cheaper postage. Postage via a courier (e.g. Evri) can work out cheaper if you live close to a parcel shop.

- Check your spellings. If you have misspelled an item or brand it will not come up on a search.

- Take pictures in daylight if you can. Artificial lights do not show colours brilliantly. Do not upload blurred pictures.

- Take pictures in a clean, tidy room. Style the area a bit, perhaps with some flowers in a vase, a nice picture in the background. Making your space look desirable, will also make the clothes look more desirable. A radiator full of wash day grey knickers or a cat litter tray in the back of your shot isn't going to make your clothes look appealing.

- Don't be greedy with pricing. However, if an item of clothing was a sell-out, or an influencer or celeb find (e.g. if Trinny

Woodall wore it on Instagram or Holly Willoughby wore it on the *This Morning* couch), you can probably get more than you originally paid as these items tend to be highly coveted. Other than that, decent quality high-street purchases tend to sell at about 30% of the original price.

SELLING HOUSEHOLD BITS

I have always been the polar opposite of a hoarder, more a compulsive declutterer. I don't feel like I can function in mess, and if I have accumulated too much stuff I start to feel disorderly and out of focus. I have always systematically sold on unused household bits, but I tended to veer toward only selling what I still thought was special. We did some renovations to the house a few years ago., and as we worked through the rooms I gathered up old fittings, naff vases, old kitchen equipment – anything that was no longer needed and that I didn't think was sellable – to take to the tip. However, before they went off to be landfill, I thought it was worth a punt to see if I could get a few quid for any of it. And, guess what? I did! What this really taught me is to never underestimate the stuff that people will buy. It may seem like worthless old tat to you, but have a go at selling on anything useable before you pile up the car with stuff for the tip.

Things I've sold

- CDs. I sent all of my CDs off to musicMagpie. I know CDs can have sentimental value, but between Spotify and YouTube every one of my CDs is online somewhere. In real life form they were just cluttering up my space. Total raised: £90.

- My old bath and sink. I kid you not, I sold it on Facebook Marketplace. Total raised: £40.
- Doors. I sold my old, battered internal house doors for £10 each on Facebook Marketplace. Total raised: £40.
- Incomplete crockery and cutlery sets. Also sold on Facebook Marketplace. Total raised: £15.
- Chinese-style teapot. Bought for 10p at a boot sale at a huge profit on Facebook Marketplace. Total raised: £20.

I think you get the gist here. It's worth having a go at selling most things before you dump them – one person's trash really is another's treasure, and you might just be getting rid of precisely the thing someone has been hunting down forever. All the while, you are making an extra bit of cash and doing your bit for the environment!

"One person's trash really is another's treasure."

I prefer to use Facebook Marketplace as impatience is one of my biggest character flaws; once I have decided something is going, I just want it gone. Marketplace is quick; there is no waiting for auctions to end, no awkward packaging required for bulky and breakable items if you make them "collection only". That said, if something is valuable it's unlikely that you are going to get as much for it on Marketplace as you would on eBay.

I recommend a six-monthly purge of rooms and cupboards to gather things to sell. It keeps me decluttered and puts some extra pennies in my bank account. It's a great rainy day boredom buster, and much better for your bank account than shopping.

CASHBACK

If you are not doing so already, make sure that you are using cashback apps and accounts. Make it your mission to see how much you could be earning back on every single thing that you buy. Cashback apps give you money back when you make purchases from participating retailers, and either require you to link your payment card or link to the retailer's website via their site or app. Every purchase that you make earns a percentage of cashback and you can let your rewards build up or withdraw them as you go. I prefer letting rewards build up so it acts as a savings account that I don't have to even pay into. I simply withdraw the funds whenever I have additional expenses.

The main UK apps are TopCashBack and Quidco. There are other apps such as loyalBe and Airtime Rewards that offer discounts off mobile phone bills or shopping vouchers.

If you are really savvy you can link a cashback bank account and stack this *on top* of the cashback reward from the site you are using.

I am not going to exhaustively list cashback providers as the market is organic in nature and new cashback apps regularly join the market. I recommend you google "Cashback Apps UK [and the current month and year]" to find out the most current, top cashback apps. There will almost always be a recent blog or article where someone else has kindly done the research legwork for you.

SHOP AROUND

If there is something that you desperately need or have been coveting and you are hell-bent on dipping into your wallet for, make sure that you do your due diligence. Being truly thrifty means exhausting every opportunity at your disposal and sourcing the most bank balance-friendly version of the thing you are hankering for. It seems like absolute common sense, but in boom times complacency kicks in and there is a tendency to take the path of least resistance and buy something quickly.

ASK FRIENDS & FAMILY

You never know what is festering unloved and unused in the cupboards, garages and attics of your friends and family. If you are looking for something practical that is not often used, like a power washer, strimmer, fondue (the list goes on), ask a friend or family member whether they have one they can loan you or that they are happy to offload for a few quid. Another great resource for one-off items can be Share and Repair shops, which offer a Library of Things; a friend used our local one to hire a chocolate fountain, a bubble machine and a gazebo for a summer party – all for less than £20.

PRICE COMPARISON SITES

It goes without saying that you should shop around and compare prices. The demise of the high street is partially due to the low overheads and reduced retail prices of internet stores. Although I lament the loss of our busy city centre, I am naturally going to buy at the lowest price possible, so even if I see something in a physical store I will use a price comparison website while in store and ask whether they can price match. In this scenario, always check out any delivery costs with the online option to establish whether it is, in fact, still cheaper to buy the online version once shipping is taken into account. The best UK comparison sites are PricerunnerUK, Idealo and PriceSpyUK, or camelcamelcamel which allows you to compare Amazon prices and get updates and alerts on price reductions.

FACTORY SECONDS & GRADED APPLIANCES

These are products that have minor or cosmetic damage and have not made it through the manufacturer's stringent quality control. They are functional and working with cosmetic defects only. I am sure most of us could live with a fridge with a slight dent on the side or a sofa with a barely visible flaw in the fabric for the sake of a few hundred quid. There are dedicated sites selling items like these – such as Factory Seconds UK, Topbrand Outlet, ElekDirect – where a middleman has bought seconds and graded products direct from factories and sites. The list of retailers is as organic as the Internet, so it is worth googling "graded appliances" if you are looking for appliances and white goods, or "factory seconds" or "outlet shop" for anything else. eBay has plenty of outlet and seconds options for furniture and homeware, such as Heals, Emma mattresses, Swoon, Rockett St George; Amazon has a dedicated Outlet Store. If you are looking for a particular retailer, refine your search to be more specific; for example, "Heals Outlet Store" or "Argos Clearance" to research cheaper alternatives to brand new prices.

SECOND-HAND SELLING PLATFORMS

We live in a throwaway culture, with clothes and shoes often being worn only a handful of times. There are thousands of items listed on selling sites as BNWT (Brand new with tags) or NWT (New without tags). If you're lusting after a particular item, it is always worth checking on eBay, Vinted or Vestiaire Collective to see if anyone is selling one. I often search on Vinted using the key phrase "this season", as it will bring up preloved (or NWT) items that are still available in the shops at full price. For example, I was yearning for a Zara dress that was £59.99 online; I searched on Vinted and bought the same dress for £20. It was in perfect condition as the seller had removed the labels, *then* tried it on and realised she'd ordered the wrong size but was unable to return it.

DUPES

I am not advocating that people purchase mass-produced fake trainers and sunglasses from sites such as Alibaba or SaraMart. I am pretty certain that the working conditions of the people making these items are dire, and they certainly don't have any cruelty-free credentials. I personally do not shop on these sites for this reason. I do, however, recommend beauty dupes from Aldi, Primark, Boots and Superdrug. Aldi dupes are remarkable, offering everything from Jo Malone-like fragrances and Charlotte Tilbury-like make-up to Olaplex-like hair care. Their products are manufactured in Europe, are cruelty-free and cost a fraction of the real deal. The quality is fantastic, and its only snobbery and ego that would make me reach for a full price, on-brand version. Similarly, Primark make-up is incredible – again cruelty-free and manufactured in the UK. They have produced almost exact dupes of Charlotte Tilbury, Estée Lauder and Dr.Jart+ products with purse-friendly price points. To find the latest dupes, check out TikTok videos – type "beauty dupes UK" in the search bar and you will be inundated with the latest offerings on the market.

TOP TAKEAWAYS
THRIFTY HABITS & STRATEGIES

- Set yourself measurable goals and try one or two of the hacks on for size. How much did you save? How did this make you feel?
- Calculate your daily disposable income.
- Break the payday millionaire cycle using the 21-day habit.
- Review your previous month's purchases against the Happiness Scale.
- Use digital pots for cash stuffing.
- Delete your debit card from your phone, Google and Apple Pay.
- Try the Monday to Wednesday Rule.
- Stretch weekly groceries out over an 8-day week.
- Use AI technology to find recipes to make meals out of leftovers.
- Try a shopping detox.
- Use cashback apps.

CHAPTER 4

GET THE FAMILY
ON BOARD

If you live in splendid isolation it's far easier to control your household budget. After all, if you are the only one using gas and electricity, eating all the snacks and adding to online shopping baskets, you've only got yourself to nag at when your bank balance is nearing zero mid-month. If, however, you share your home with children, a partner, relatives or housemates, it's a good idea to get everyone on board with making changes to save pennies that can soon add up into pounds. Adults, theoretically, should be easier to negotiate with and convince to adopt a thriftier lifestyle. Children are expensive little housemates with no concept that living costs money – as such, they require a unique set of tactics to get them involved.

Whatever stage you are at in navigating parenthood, you will always think it's the toughest. We have a tendency to wish a seemingly difficult stage away, wistfully yearning for the part where it gets easy. This is not a book about parenting, but the hard truth (from a mother to teens) is that it doesn't get easier, it's just different! You need to be on the front foot, constantly renewing your parenting toolkit and tactics to support, guide, negotiate and corral our precious offspring through babyhood, the toddler years, adolescence, and – with the cost of living the way it is – probably through their twenties when they're still living at home. Personally, I think a two-year-old's tantrum in Tesco is a walk in the park compared to a belligerent teen who, despite their limited time on Earth, knows everything and thinks you possess all the common sense of a badger crossing a motorway.

"Living with less and cutting your cloth requires the whole family to be mindful of what's being consumed and what is being spent."

Why am I sharing this? Well, living with less and cutting your cloth requires the whole family to be mindful of what's being consumed and what is being spent. Engaging kids in thrifty thinking from a young age will save you pennies, pounds and hours of frustrated nagging. I have broken down the tactics you can use to reduce your child's carbon footprint by age group, with lots of tips and hints that will save you money along the way.

THE BABY STAGE

Babies don't make any decisions for themselves. Everything that you do, purchase and use to keep them safe, happy, fed and warm is down to you. When you are expecting baby number one, retailers' marketing is aimed to target every single one of your doubts, fears and insecurities about impending parenthood. Marketing is designed to exploit your love for your child and make you feel that your devotion is measured in how well equipped you are with expensive and fancy baby paraphernalia. Babies like to be warm, feel loved and safe and have full bellies. Humans have been reproducing since we were cave dwellers, and we have done a pretty good job at surviving over hundreds of thousands of years without gadgets and gizmos to keep baby happy.

Put simply, you don't need 80% of the stuff you buy for a new baby. Although Kim Kardashian and Beyoncé may beg to differ, a new baby doesn't need a £8,000 top of the range acrylic crib; your love doesn't correlate directly into what you spend on stuff for them. Anyone that has had a second child will quickly tell you that they didn't buy half of the unnecessary stuff for the second baby, as you recognise it just isn't needed. Marketing moguls have a very short window to lure you in: first baby, pre-birth and first year; and they do everything they can to exploit your insecurities and lack of knowledge and experience to part you from your hard-earned cash.

BUY PRELOVED CLOTHES

Babies grow like grass. Stocking up on a few new onesies and vests pre-birth is understandable, but I can guarantee that a lot of clothes you buy new will not get worn. Car boot sales and charity shops are awash with baby clothes in excellent condition – if not new with tags – as they are often never worn or used for a very brief time. Even kinder on the wallet than preloved clothes are hand me downs. Don't be afraid to ask friends and family with older children if they would let you make use of anything their child has outgrown; and, of course, make sure you look after them so you can offer them back if they have another child.

BUGGIES

Buying a buggy, if you are lucky, is sometimes the domain of the grandparents, who are often very keen to treat you to a new, top of the range buggy to transport your precious cargo around town. You will spend hours agonising over the latest designs and newest, snazziest buggies on the market – but they all do the same thing. Having the very latest, trendiest buggy is a vanity thing – you can rock up at baby group and steal the show with the bells and whistles buggy of the year. Your baby won't care. Honestly, you are much better buying a preloved buggy in good condition or choosing a mid-range affordable buggy and investing any surplus that you would have spent in an ISA or trust fund for your child.

BABY BOOKS

Unfortunately, these pesky human babies do not come with an instruction manual. In an effort to perfect solid and controllable baby routines, sleeping patterns and nutrition, we buy baby books in volumes to guide us through the uncertainty. The window for new parents needing these guides and manuals is brief, as we quickly realise there is no perfect parent formula and you have to work with your own child and family routines. As a result, charity shops and car boot sales are awash with abandoned parenting books for as little as 50p.

BATH TIME

The majority of parenting books talk about "routine", and I fell into the trap of bathing my little ones daily before bedtime because I felt like I had to have a routine in pursuit of the Holy Grail, aka a solid night's sleep. But what happened? Both of my small people developed eczema in my pursuit of the perfect bath time, bedtime routine. Of course, when bathing a baby, the water and bathroom needs to be toasty warm, which uses energy and water. In reality, the National Childbirth Trust states that babies don't actually need a bath daily – a couple of times a week will do the trick, along with daily top-to-toe flannel washes. Reducing the amount of baths will save you energy and water (and help prevent your precious bundle's skin from drying out).

FOOD

Jars of baby food are convenient but expensive. The cheapest way to feed baby is to adapt your family meal portions and blend a portion of your supper or lunch for baby. This gets baby used to lots more flavours and trains them to enjoy the food the rest of the family eats. Just make sure you reduce the salt content; you can always add salt to the adult meals once the baby's portion has been removed.

> **"Leftover veggies are great to use in homemade baby foods and a great way to reduce food waste."**

You can also easily batch cook baby meals and freeze portions to use as needed. Leftover veggies are great to use in homemade baby foods and a great way to reduce food waste. You don't need to buy and prepare fancy ingredients, and it saves on packaging.

NAPPIES

Oh my goodness! The relief when you no longer have to add nappies to the weekly shopping basket. They are pricey, and that cost only increases as your precious poppet moves up through the sizes. Reusable nappies are a great alternative, and not as gross as they sound as you use liners with them to absorb lots of the poop. Some local councils run voucher schemes where they will subsidise your first pack of reusable nappies. It might seem surprising, but buying reusable nappy kits will save you thousands of pounds and reduce the amount of waste baby produces dramatically. If reusable are not for you (and they aren't for many), then supermarket own brand nappies are just as good as the expensive leading brands and will save you a pretty penny in the long run.

FREE STUFF

Get your mitts on all the freebies you can for baby. All of the leading baby manufacturers of food, nappies, wipes, creams, potions and lotions want you to try their stuff and then ultimately start buying it. Emmasdiary.co.uk is a good source of information AND freebies, but all of the big manufacturers have baby clubs that you can sign up for: Optimal, Johnson's, Huggies, Pampers, Boots, MAM, Ella's Kitchen to name a few. Make hunting for freebies and money-off coupons your low-energy activity while baby is napping.

GROUPS & ACTIVITIES

Baby yoga anyone? You and your baby are an opportunity for people to make money. There are lots of mother and baby activity franchises that pop up depending on what is in vogue. Hands down nothing beats the local free Rhyme Time in your library or the local church hall mother and baby groups that cost pennies for an afternoon of play, chat and coffee. These low-cost groups give you the opportunity to see how your child interacts with new toys and gauge what they will actually want to play with before investing in toys for home too. I still consider the women that I met in local church hall play groups to be my closest friends, and the children still reunite for "Playgroup Friends Beach Days". You don't need expensive memberships and groups to make lifelong connections and socialise your little ones.

YOUNG CHILDREN (2–7 YEARS)

Apart from the odd toddler meltdown, young children are quite malleable. They are eager to please and believe what you tell them... It is a magical and precious time, and it's your window of opportunity to get them into good habits around waste and spending (your money of course)! There are lots of videos and resources online (YouTube) to support educating younger children about energy use and fossil fuels. Helping them to understand that resources are finite, whether it be fossil fuels or your hard-earned moolah, will go a long way in getting them involved in living less wastefully.

TOYS

The adverts for and packaging on toys hold so much promise for little people. Despite gargantuan technological advances in recent decades, most analogue toys are still inanimate plastic, overpriced tat. That doesn't stop kids wanting them though – and it doesn't stop you wanting to keep them happy by providing them with said toys. However, visit any car boot sale up and down the land and 60% of what is on offer is lightly used games and toys and teddy bears. From a very young age, my kids would get up with me on a Sunday morning and come to a car boot sale. It was a fun morning out and they had a modest budget for new toys. Although young, they soon learned to haggle and how to budget. They would leave clutching mint condition toys that would have cost an arm and a leg new. A wipe down with disinfectant or a quick whizz in the washing machine and most things come up good as new. Younger kids don't compare themselves to others, and mine never baulked at having preloved toys; and helping children to understand that plastic is damaging to wildlife and the environment is a good way to engage them in an early love of preloved goods. If they have a favourite animal, you can talk about its natural habitat and the dangers that manufacturing brings to that animal's world; this context brings the issues to life for them.

CLOTHES & DRESS-UP

There isn't an awful lot of variety on the high street for kid's clothes nowadays, so again using charity shops and car boot sales to buy preloved children's clothes will save you a fortune – and there is always a lot on offer simply because they grow out of things so quickly. And you can resell them on once yours have outgrown them. I regularly complete a wardrobe cull and sell bundles on Facebook Marketplace and they literally fly out. I reuse the money I have raised to buy replacement items at the car boot sale, keeping their clothes circular and out of the waste stream as well as saving money.

World Book Day... three words that make every parent's blood run cold, especially at 9pm on a Sunday evening. If I had a quid for every Harry Potter outfit I've seen hanging up in a charity shop I'd be shopping at Waitrose. Don't waste your money on expensive dressing-up outfits, the charity shops and car boot sales and even Facebook Marketplace have plenty on offer at a fraction of the price. If your child has an abstract imagination and demands an outfit from an obscure book, get creative with adapting charity shop clothes, bedding and accessories to make a sustainable and cheaper alternative.

WHEELIE GOOD

There is such joy in seeing your precious little bundle progress from being a baby, to walking to mastering the art of scooters, trikes, bikes and go karts. The trouble is they keep growing, and you have to keep replacing said wheeled toy with an appropriate-sized vehicle. This is expensive and, depending on how fast your child grows, really wasteful. For every wheeled toy upgrade you need, there is a parent out there doing the very same – so, again, buying preloved is a far more sensible option. As the days get longer and the weather brightens, people start to sort out garages and sheds, making spring a great time to bag a Marketplace or Gumtree bargain bike or scooter. You may also have a local bicycle refurbish scheme; we have a local charity that refurbishes and services bikes and scooters for resale at affordable prices. It's worth investigating whether your locality has something similar as part of your council's low carbon initiative. Again, once outgrown these can be resold so you are always trading up using the existing toy to part-find its replacement.

SNACKS & DRINKS ON THE GO

Kids don't need a constant stream of snacks and drinks the minute they leave the house. As long as they have had their breakfast they should be good for a few hours. That said, the minute we piled into the car or headed to the park, my little darlings would be foraging in my bag for "snack". Anywhere you go that is geared up for kids entertainment will charge a premium for food and drink: soft play, cinema, cafés. Always take your own snacks to get children into the habit early of not expecting overpriced café snacks and drinks. Encourage them to help pack their snack choices at home. We always used little sandwich bags and wrote their names on them so that they had a snack attack pack each. Choosing the contents themselves helped to alleviate any nagging for a café snack as they had already picked their favourite sandwich fillings and drinks from home and looked forward to the snacks they had helped to make.

BATHS & SHOWERS

Echoing what was said for babies, unless your child has painted themselves Smurf blue from head to toe in nursery or rolled in mud like a truffle-hunting pig, there really is no pressing need to bathe or shower young children daily. Scaling back from daily scrubbing will save you energy and water. Once your child has progressed into the bathing unaccompanied stage, it's worth introducing them to the world of the shower. It uses both less energy and water, and you can get snazzy shower timers to engage them in saving water. My kids responded really well to the beating the timer game, and even tried to outdo each other to see who could get showered the quickest (they are still ridiculously competitive)! Instilling these habits at a young age sets the scene and makes it easier for you to save energy as they get older.

ENERGY SAVING

Younger children respond really well to praise and reward, and star charts and reward charts are really popular ways of engaging them. Using YouTube videos and online resources to explain that things need electricity to work, and helping them to understand that this costs money, is a great way to engage them in energy saving around the house. At bedtime, you can ask them to help you find things that can be switched off in their bedroom, and to turn off lights, TVs, games consoles, etc. as part of their bedtime routine. You can award stars for each appliance that they remember to switch off, which can be exchanged for a treat at the end of the week. You can do this in other rooms in the home too, and ask them to help you look for things that can be switched off.

"Use YouTube videos and online resources to explain to children that things need electricity to work."

It goes without saying that younger children shouldn't be touching plug sockets, but they can help you to identify where appliances and gadgets can be switched off when they are not being used.

If you have a smart meter to measure your electricity usage, introduce your children to it: show them the numbers and explain that it goes red when something costs a lot of money. Kids will assume that, like the air we breathe, all of the energy that they use "just is"; they don't know it comes with a price attached, so gently getting them to understand that there is a finite amount that you can use within your budget is a great way to explain the numbers. Explain that if it gets to £7 (or whatever your budget is) a day, that's all that we can use. You can use coins to demonstrate and tally with the smart meter numbers to show them how it adds up, correlating the coins with devices and gadgets that use energy.

Smart meters

Lots of people are suspicious of smart meters, but all they do is tell you exactly what you have consumed daily. The energy doesn't cost you more. There is no catch – actually, it puts you in control. I opted for an additional in-home display unit with an app that provides me with data, intelligence and insights into what I am spending money on each month.

KEEPING WARM

Kids love to move and kids like your undivided attention. A way of keeping warm while entertaining and engaging with them and getting your daily steps in is to dance. Stick on some tunes and make up silly dances together. It will keep you warm for ages, and I guarantee the music that you pick will be interwoven into some of your happiest memories. Music and moving is good for the soul. If you struggle physically, you can adapt to your ability – but any movement will make you warmer.

SANTA CLAUS, THE TOOTH FAIRY & THE EASTER BUNNY

Set the scene early for Santa only bringing one special gift for kids; let them know that Santa doesn't bring all of their Christmas gifts. When times are hard and you are budgeting, it's much harder to explain why Santa didn't struggle down the chimney with the vast mountain of toys that he did in previous years. This gives you wiggle room for explaining that parents have a budget and that they will still get a lovely gift off Santa, and mummy and daddy will buy what they can afford. The same principle applies to any other fabled character that brings kids gifts. Set the bar early: the Tooth Fairy brings £1, the Easter Bunny brings one egg. Manage expectations from an early age.

PRE-TEENS & TEENS

Pre-teens and teens have slightly more autonomy – and definitely more opinions. Once you hit the teenage years, you will find your kids want to stay up later than you at weekends, are constantly snuffling for snacks, and are capable of preparing quick, easy meals unsupervised. Teenagers don't listen to you – because you know nothing, and they, on the other hand, know everything. They are, however, still reasonably mouldable into good habits with some basic house rules. With older kids, there is the added bug bear that they notice what others have and start comparing themselves to their peers. They will nag for mobile phones and games consoles, and toys progress from being cheaper "small world"-type toys to being more expensive electricals. School homework is predominantly online, which means they will almost probably need a laptop, notebook or tablet to access homework.

ELECTRONICS

Laptops, mobile phones, games consoles and tablets do not come cheap and, whether we like it or not, they are part of modern life. In the sticky hands of a clumsy pre-teen the chances of them getting damaged are high. Handing a child a £1,000 tablet is far too much responsibility for them to be saddled with, even if you do teach them to look after and respect their belongings. There are plenty of retailers who sell preowned refurbished (with warranties) devices online (such as backmarket.co.uk, reboxed. co.uk, musicmagpie.co.uk). And if you use your credit card to make the purchase, you have the added assurance of the card provider having an equal responsibility with the seller if anything goes wrong with the purchase. I am reticent to buy electricals from Facebook Marketplace or Gumtree as there is no comeback if anything goes wrong, and there are so many scams. It is also worth contacting your local authority, school or library to see if you have a local digital inclusion scheme where surplus tablets and laptops are redistributed to families that may be digitally excluded.

MEALS & SNACKS

As a "feeder", I have been guilty of buying treats and snacks to make the kids happy, but once on a much more restricted budget

I stopped buying them. Apart from the health benefits of not munching through fatty, high calorie, non-nutritious snacks, these extras add a substantial whack on to your weekly shopping bill. Do you know what happened? No one complained, they actually finished their proper meals and we wasted less food. An extra snack is now a bowl of cereal: it doesn't require energy to cook, we have it in the cupboard anyway, and it's filling and not terrible for your kid's health. I have saved at least a tenner on the cost of my weekly shop by curbing the crisps and snacks.

CURFEW

Pre-teens' bedtime is relatively easy to manage, as they generally go to bed before you; you tuck them in and it's lights out. Then there is a strange shift once they hit the teen years; you find yourself yawning on the sofa in front of Netflix at 9.30pm while the teens seem to get a second wind. On many nights I've been tucked up in my fleece bedding and the kids are roaming the house, Snapchatting pals, air frying freezer food, microwaving canned goodies and cremating toast – all of which uses energy. I introduced a Wi-Fi curfew, as it is access to online entertainment that holds most appeal for nocturnal older kids; TV streaming, group chats and scrolling TikTok are all a distraction from sleeping. Adding parental controls that cull access to anything online, or simply switching off the Wi-Fi at a specific time, mean that there is nothing for them to do except homework or read a book – neither of which is as appealing to the majority of teens as being online. Mine simply retreated to bed defeated, which meant our daily energy use instantly went down by about £1.

POCKET MONEY

Pocket money is a good way to teach kids to budget – when it's gone it's gone. Whatever your personal budget, allocating money for pocket money each month means that you can avoid them asking for money throughout the month. I guarantee that if you choose to spot them a fiver here and there rather than give a regular allowance, it will cost you more overall. Earning pocket money is another great way to encourage kids to get on board with valuing the money they have and with helping out around the house and energy saving. We have a points for pounds system in our home and have built in energy saving into the pocket money that the kids can earn.

- Tidy bedroom, including rehanging clothes that can be worn again and not throwing them in the laundry: 25p per day.
- Getting up, dressed and out the house with no backchat or stalling: 25p per day.
- Turning all games consoles, TVs, plug sockets off at night: 25p per day.
- 5-minute showering: 25p per day.
- Completing homework: 25p per day
- Household chores: 25p per day

So in total they can earn £1.50 per day or £10.50 per week.

You can adjust the amounts to suit the child's age, needs and your budget, but it's the allocation of simple tasks to points and money that works. If they don't manage to complete the task, they get the day's allocation deducted. It's a great way to get them into good habits, make them aware of the energy they use, as well as managing some of the issues we prickle over regularly in the home. The hanging and spritzing with antibacterial fabric spray of clothes that have been worn once has reduced our laundry from two loads per day to three loads per week, saving me a substantial amount on detergent, energy and water.

SHOWERS OVER BATHS

Showers are a cheaper option to a bath, so transitioning kids to taking a quick shower is a no-brainer. The important word here is "quick". Older kids don't respond well to games like egg timers and shower races, and a long hot shower feels so good, of course they are going to want to stand in there for 10 minutes. If you own a teen, it may be all you can do to get them into the shower; but once they are in there, it's great to get them into good habits by limiting themselves to a 5-minute shower. They don't have the life experience that we do and, as silly as it sounds, explaining what to do when they get in there is a must. We just assume that they know, but explaining that you don't just stand there enjoying the warm water and that you have to wash and rinse to get the job done is important. Building a 5-minute shower into the pocket money points is a great way to get them on board with embracing a quick shower.

ADULTS

Unless you have been living under a rock, we all know that energy costs more than it did a couple of years ago. It can still be testing to get adults, whether it be partners, housemates and adult kids living at home to get involved with being thrifty. I have led the way in our household, but it hasn't been without some persuasion. A smart meter is a must to keep tabs and demonstrate why the air fryer is the better option, or why showering at the gym (even if it's more of a faff) makes sense. Compiling an Energy Use table (See Chapter 5, Thrifty Energy Use) is a really useful way to demonstrate exactly what everything costs per 10 minutes and per hour; it brings the cost of electricity to life, and gives you foresight so that you can negotiate new ways of doing things in the home.

TOP TAKEAWAYS
GET THE FAMILY ON BOARD

- Buy preloved wherever you can: baby equipment, clothes, toys, dress-up clothes, games consoles, laptops, mobile phones, tablets, etc. You will save an absolute fortune, as well as preventing already manufactured stuff from going to landfill or being incinerated.
- Sign up for free stuff for babies and children online – there are lots of parenting sites and even companies that give away free stuff for little people.
- Always pack your own snacks and picnics for days out for younger children, and get them involved in preparing their own snack pack.
- Limit between-meal snacks for older kids. Stop buying the unhealthy crisps and sweet snacks. Their teeth and health and your weekly food budget will all benefit.

- Make saving energy fun for little ones using a star reward system and introducing shower timers to make taking a quick shower a game. Use online resources to help them understand that resources are not finite.
- Move, dance to music, be silly, play games that involve moving to help to stay warm.
- Introduce Wi-Fi curfews to limit how long older kids stay up at night.
- Use pocket money as a way to introduce children to budgeting. and weave in rewards for energy saving and household chores.
- Use your smart meter to get kids on board with understanding that energy isn't free.
- Make finding opportunities to save money something you all get a dopamine hit from. Reward and praise any great ideas that your children have.

CHAPTER 5

THRIFTY ENERGY USE

Here is the brutal truth: there is not much you can do to save energy except to use less of it.

As energy costs per kWh are through the roof, energy usage is the one area where some simple switches can save you some serious cash. Finding less energy-greedy ways of doing things and making some compromises on how you live is vital if you're cash-strapped. Remember, small changes soon add up; and the compound impact of lots of small savings on energy is a big monthly decrease in your energy costs. According to the energy market intelligence provider Cornwall Insight, 1 in 5 UK households are in fuel poverty in 2023. Although my tone may be light-hearted, the message most certainly isn't.

"There is not much you can do to save energy except to use less of it."

Saving money on energy feels very different in August to what it does in December. There is no getting around it; winter energy saving does take some grit and does require that the big person pants are firmly hoisted up. However, there are some things that you can do all year round that will make a huge difference to your energy.

In this chapter, I will walk you through how to energy audit your home: identify the energy-guzzling devices and the swaps you can make; and offer some nifty hacks that can help save you money on your energy bills. You can pick and choose the things that work best for your household. Ever the scrooge, I have tried all of these hacks, but the first step is always foresight.

GAIN FORESIGHT & TAKE CONTROL

As soon as the energy crisis hit I knew I needed to feel like I had some control. There is nothing worse than feeling "hard done by" – it breaks your resolve before you have even started. Control means that you see opportunities, rather than problems. Feeling a degree of control helps you be more resilient in the face of change. The first thing I did when the energy crisis hit was audit every single appliance in my home so that I could discover what was on the "OMG! How much an hour?" list and what was on the "OK. We can live with that list".

"This is about being able to tighten your belt when you need to, and then squeezing that extra little bit when your bank account is screaming for help."

The energy crisis will eventually lose its zeitgeist-like name as we all become numbed to it being a crisis, and it will become the norm. Nevertheless, I highly recommend doing an energy audit so you can take back control and spend less on energy usage in your home whatever the state of the energy markets. This is about being able to tighten your belt when you need to, and then squeezing that extra little bit when your bank account is screaming for help.

THE ENERGY AUDIT

Which appliances do you use in your home? It's not something you really stop to think about, but knowledge is power – and it is also going to help you to make smarter choices so your money stays in your bank account instead of lining some energy fat cat's wallet. I started by dividing the appliances that we own and use into categories:

- kitchen
- utility room
- entertainment
- heating & drying
- beauty & bathroom

I then wandered around the house like a building inspector, clipboard in hand, recording all the gadgets and gizmos. Breaking it down into sections makes it much less of an overwhelming task, and it also comes in handy for the savings overhaul which we will cover in this chapter.

The next thing to do is to create a table/spreadsheet. There are energy audit templates in the back of the book you can copy, and below are examples of my audits. All of the prices are based on the April 2023 Energy Unit price cap, but you will need to recalculate as costs go up and down. The point of this exercise is to demonstrate where you could make some hefty savings around your home. These pounds soon add up and, if nothing else, help in the battle against rising costs. Whatever your current situation, your money is better off in your bank account ready to be spent on the things that bring you joy rather than being drained by the appliances in your home.

I searched online to identify the wattages of my appliances and gadgets – the manufacturer's specification will give this information. Don't worry if your slow cooker is as old as God's dog and was invented before the Internet, you can google the typical wattage and use that.

To get the energy prices, I use a free online energy calculator on www.sust-it.net/energy-calculator.php, mostly because it's foolproof and I get a mental block when I am faced with tricky maths challenges. It's all pre-set with the current prices per unit and you can check cost in minutes and hours. I recorded in the audit the cost for both 10 minutes and an hour, because that helps me to decide most easily which energy-saving swaps I can make.

IN THE KITCHEN

Kitchen			
Appliance	Wattage	Cost per hour	Cost per 10 mins
Kettle	3000	£1.02	17p
Hob	2000	68p	11p
Electric grill	1500	51p	8p

Appliance	Wattage	Cost per hour	Cost per 10 mins
Panini/Toastie maker	1500	51p	8p
Air fryer	1500	51p	8p
Halogen oven	1300	44p	7p
George Foreman grill	1200	41p	7p
InSinkErator tap	1200	41p	7p
Toaster	1000	34p	6p
Pressure cooker	700	24p	4p
Blender	600	20p	3p
Slow cooker	350	12p	2p
Extractor fan	35	1p	0.2p

As fridges and freezers cycle on and off, it is difficult to gauge an hourly cost so they haven't been included. You might have noticed the hum from them when they are running; that's the compressor making sure they reach the right cooled temperature so, in short, they are not on for a full hour. And in reality you are not going to switch them off anyway or your food would end up a festering mess. If you are in the market for a replacement, be mindful of buying an A-rated efficient one. If you are not, don't worry as I have got some hacks for reducing running costs later in this chapter.

Appliance wars

To get an idea of the energy cost of cooking a family meal, I've prepared audits of a couple of family meals cooked using different appliances.

Casseroles and stews are great ways of using up any veg festering in the veg drawer of the fridge; most kids like them, and they are hearty, filling and cheap to make. But, there are a variety of ways you can cook them; and this is where costs can differ significantly.

Method of cooking casserole	Time to cook	Cooking cost
Oven	3 hrs	**£2.16**
Hob	3 hrs	**£2.04**
Slow cooker	6 hrs	**72p**
Pressure cooker	40 mins	**16p**

Based on April 2023 Prices

As you can see, if you have a pressure cooker (maybe an old relic from the 1980s lurking at the back of your cupboard), you could be quids in. Switching your oven for the pressure cooker gives you a whopping 93% saving per meal. The slow cooker coming in second cheapest, with a saving of 67% compared to the oven.

Another typical midweek meal might be chicken, potato wedges and peas – quick and easy to prepare, but what's the most cost-efficient way of cooking it?

Method, time & cost for cooking chicken & wedges	Method, time & cost for cooking peas	Total cooking cost
Oven 40 mins (10 mins to heat oven) 48p	Hob 10 mins 11p	**59p**
Air fryer 25 mins 21p	Microwave 4 mins 0.03p	**21.3p**

Method, time & cost for cooking chicken & wedges	Method, time & cost for cooking peas	Total cooking cost
Smaller air fryer (wedges) 20 mins 16p George Foreman grill (chicken) 12 mins 8p Total: 24p	Microwave 4 mins 0.03p	24.3p

These tables give you an idea of how to plan your cooking and meals around energy-efficient appliances, using the cheapest and quickest methods possible to cook meals. NB: If you are cooking a feast like a Christmas dinner, you will need a bigger oven as a turkey won't fit in most air fryers.

If you are looking for new appliances for the kitchen, this way of calculating costs can also help you to make really informed choices on what to invest in if you are serious about making long-term savings. While you may not be in the fortunate position to go crazy on the Argos app, preloved, well-looked-after alternatives can be found on Facebook Marketplace and Gumtree. I bought my slow cooker at a car boot sale for £3 five years ago and it's still going strong. Always check items are working first and hygienic. You can pretty much tell from someone's house whether they are likely to have maintained it and kept it clean from the state of their kitchen. Ask them to demo it indoors so you can make your mind up. If the kitchen is sparkling and you would accept a cuppa from them and it works, all is good. If the sink is piled up and they've added the cat litter tray and kids' potty to the washing up, then it's safe to say it might not be a goer.

THE REST OF THE HOME

I worked my way through the house room by room, populating my list and working out costs.

Utility Room			
Appliance	**Wattage**	**Cost per hour**	**Cost per 10 mins**
Immersion heater	3000	£1.02	17p
Tumble dryer	2500	85p	14p
Dishwasher	2400	82p	14p
Washing machine	1500	51p	8p
Clothes steamer	1600	54p	9p
Iron	1500	51p	8p
Vacuum cleaner (plug-in)	1000	34p	6p
Vacuum cleaner (cordless)	200	7p	1p

Entertainment			
Appliance	**Wattage**	**Cost per hour**	**Cost per 10 mins**
PlayStation	145	5p	0.8p
X Box	95	3p	0.5p
Nintendo Switch	10	0.2p	0.03p
Plasma TV	110	4p	0.6p
Sound bar speaker	35	1p	0.2p
CRT TV	90	3p	0.5p
OLED TV	60	2p	0.3p
Desktop PC	100	3p	0.5p

Appliance	Wattage	Cost per hour	Cost per 10 mins
Laptop	50	1.5p	0.25p
Monitor LCD 17-inch	20	0.5p	0.08p
Monitor LED 17-inch	18	0.5p	0.08p
Wi-Fi Mesh system	11	0.37p	
Sewing machine	100	3p	0.5p
Standard light bulb	60	2p	0.33p
LED lightbulb	9	0.31p	0.05p
Charging smartphone	4	0.11p	0.03p

Heating & drying			
Appliance	Wattage	Cost per hour	Cost per 10 mins
Gas boiler	24kW	£2.40 at 10p kWh for gas	n/a
Fan heater	3000	£1.02	17p
Storage heating	1500	51p	7p
Oil-filled heater	1500	51p	8p
Halogen heater	1000	34p	6p
Calor gas heater	15kg lasts 50hrs = £48		
Open fire	Depends on fuel and local costs		
Dehumidifier	400	14p	2p
Electric blanket (bed)	200	7p	1p
Heated towel rail	200	7p	1p
Heated clothes airer	200	7p	1p
Heated throw	85	3p	0.5p
Air purifier	50	1.5p	0.25p

Beauty			
Appliance	**Wattage**	**Cost per hour**	**Cost per 10 mins**
Hairdryer	2000	68p	11p
Straighteners	200	7p	1p
Tongs	200	7p	1p

Bathroom energy costs October 2022		
Energy required to heat 1 litre of water: 0.4kWh		
Electric cost to heat 1 litre of water = 34p per kWh/0.4 = 0.85p per litre		
Gas cost to heat 1 litre of water = 10p per kWh/0.04 = 0.25p		
Gas		
Bath 80 litres	20p	
Shower 6 litres per minute	7.5p (5 mins/30 litres)	15p (10 mins/60 litres)

ENERGY-SAVING HACKS

I know I sound like a stuck record, but the only way to save money on energy is to **USE LESS**. I've got a whole host of easy hacks that are not too painful – you won't have to live like a 17th-century pauper. It just takes a bit of planning and thinking – but you are half way there with your lists.

I'll walk you through the sections on the home audit and you can pick and choose which hacks work for you. I saved £50 a month as soon as I started making these changes.

COOKING

Hopefully, at this point, you've done a bit of an audit of your appliances and are giving your oven the side eye. Ovens use a lot of energy and take an age to heat up. You waste the first 10 minutes just getting the damned thing hot enough to cook in. You know what I mean: you look at the cooking instructions on a pack of nuggets and automatically add 10 minutes to the cooking time or else find yourself chomping into soggy half-cooked reformed chicken.

I stopped using my oven completely bar the one time when I misguidedly thought I'd use it to cook some of Aldi's premium range sausages. They took an hour – never again. And my oven is only three years old. I have switched my oven for much cheaper-to-run appliances and plan my meals around them.

MAKE THE MOST OF SUNNY DAYS

If you have an outdoor barbecue use it in the summer. If you have the gas already it's essentially free; if you were going to buy gas or charcoal anyway, you may as well take advantage of the blink-and-you-miss-it summer to cook and eat outdoors. Salads are for the most part cook-free, and even buying a supermarket rotisserie chicken and opening a bag of mixed leaves is cheaper than buying and cooking the chicken yourself.

SWITCH THE OVEN FOR AN AIR FRYER

The air fryer is just a mini-oven that sits on your counter top. But – and it's a big but – it heats up quicker than a regular oven and cooks things in half the time. Oven chips crispy and perfect in 10 minutes rather than the painful 20 minutes in the oven which still leaves a few soggy stragglers in the tray. Using the oven every night for 30 minutes costs

£131 a year; 30 minutes' air fryer usage (mine's 1500W) costs £91 – a saving of £40 a year already. And if you halve the cooking time, that's another £20 saved. So switching to an air fryer can save you £60 a year (minus the upfront costs if you haven't got one, of course!).

I hear you muttering, but I can't afford an air fryer. I recommend you look at the purchase as a long-term investment. If energy prices go up but your wages don't, the savings will become even more apparent. As unglamorous as it sounds, it's an ideal birthday or Christmas gift (if anyone can still afford gifts that is); or you can pick them up preloved on Marketplace and Gumtree; or use supermarket loyalty rewards to buy one. You could also ask friends and family if they have any old appliances going begging, and drop it in conversation at work or at the school gates that you are looking for one; or put a call out for a free one on local Freecycle and Don't Dump It groups. Drop your pride and get your hustle on – there will be a second-hand air fryer out there somewhere with your name on it.

DIG OUT OLD FRIENDS

Have a rummage in the backs of cupboards, or the attic or garage, or wherever you store unused stuff in your house. A few years back, "health grills" named after famous boxers had their day in the spotlight, as did the pressure cooker that every upwardly mobile family had in the 1980s. These appliances both cook quickly, and cooking quicker at a lower wattage is where the magic is.

I use my health grill a lot. After festering unloved in the pan drawer for a few years, I realised it could save me some serious cash. The key to speeding up cooking even further is to slice thicker cuts (like chicken breasts or sausages) down the middle to create thinner fillets. Cutting them in half literally halves the cooking time.

Let's look at the health grill cost compared to the demon oven…

My last sausage experiment in the oven took an hour to get them browned enough for my liking. I'm not a fan of a pink sausage – I immediately hear my mum telling me that uncooked pork will give me worms and a childhood trauma induced meltdown results. They take seven minutes on the health grill when cut in half. Now, food purists and chefs might be sucking their teeth at me, but this is a book about saving money, not creating Michelin-starred delights.

"Switching appliances in the kitchen is a really easy way to save on cooking costs."

So let's do the maths on that. If sausages take an hour in the oven, if you ate them every night for a year it would cost £262.80. If you cooked them on the health grill it would be £18.25 over the year. I don't know anyone who *would* eat sausages every night, but the savings are obvious.

THE HOB

This is another kitchen demon, operating at around 2000 Watts. We use it mainly for stir fries as they cook so quickly – 10 minutes and you are done, so that's only about 11p to cook. If you are using the hob to stew, I would suggest using a slow cooker instead. If you are cooking frozen veg, get the portion out of the freezer first thing in the morning and defrost it all day so you are just warming it rather than cooking from frozen. Even better, defrost it in the morning and use a microwave, which is generally a much lower wattage.

TOP TAKEAWAYS
COOKING ENERGY-SAVING HACKS

- Switch energy-hungry appliances for cheaper-to-run appliances.
- Batch cook where you can – you can use two Maggi bags or buy special slow cooker bags. Two meals – one slow cooker (see page 137 for more tips on this).
- Plan meals around how you will cook them (more on this in Chapter 6).
- Try and cook things as quickly as possible, or use a slow cooker. Defrost everything (from chops to pizzas) thoroughly as they will cook quicker than from frozen.
- Cut meat in half to make thinner, quicker to cook fillets.
- Look for good preloved energy-efficient appliances online; or beg, borrow or loan from friends, family and neighbours.
- Bring out of retirement any old energy-efficient appliances, such as health grills and pressure cookers, you may have.
- Use your barbecue and eat pre-cooked meats and salads in summer.

THE FRIDGE

Your fridge circulates cool air and works hard to maintain a nice cool temperature. Any help that you can give your fridge to stay cool will mean the compressor doesn't have to work as hard, saving you money. Plan ahead and defrost frozen food in the fridge and you are effectively cooling it for free. Make sure your fridge isn't packed to the rafters, as you need space to circulate the cool air. Also, you can turn down the temperature in the fridge when the air drops cold in your kitchen as this is when your fridge isn't battling to maintain cold temperatures.

LAUNDRY DAY

When my kids were small, my laundry basket seemed to be constantly full, and the washer and drier were on at least once a day; I would wistfully look forward to them being teenagers, when the laundry basket would be empty and I could give up my full-time laundry assistant role. What a fool I was! Fast-forward to them being teens and they continue to generate heaps of laundry, only now the clothes are bigger so it's MORE to wash.

The easiest way to save money on laundry is to do less of it, but you don't have to smell like Stig of the Dump in the process. Before the cost of living crisis hit, I didn't give using my washing machine and tumble drier much thought. Getting clothes dry is so damned expensive, but without a tumble drier, drying is its own very special kind of hell. But don't worry – help is at hand.

WASH LESS

How many dutiful mums out there have placed a neatly folded pile of clean laundry on their kid's bed for them to put away... and then found the exact same items of clothes back in the wash basket the next day, just because your little darling couldn't be arsed to hang them up? We got into bad habits in our family when money wasn't as tight: one wear and clothes were washed. Not only did this mean that clothes faded and wore out quicker, it added to the relentless grind of never-ending laundry. Now energy prices have risen, I do a wash every three days for a family of three. How do I do it you ask?

SNIFF & SPRAY

Simple and effective! As you are gathering clothing up from the bed, floor, basket or the back of the gaming chair, sniff them (maybe not boys' socks – they will strip the hairs off from up your nose!). If there is a vague aroma of detergent or fabric softener, it's fresh as a daisy and will do another couple of wears; so stick it on a hanger and pop it back in the wardrobe. If it smells clean but not washday fresh, give it a spritz with an antibacterial clothes spray.

I do this with my own clothes; as I'm getting ready for bed, I give them a quick sniff and a good old spray, paying attention to armpits and crotch areas, and then hang them straight back in my wardrobe. It's bacteria that makes clothes smell of sweat, so antibac spray freshens them and makes them fit to see another day. You can also spritz your bedding and towels to extend the time between washes. I am a Fabulosa Spray and Wear evangelist; it costs a quid and comes in many lovely scents (baby powder is my all-time favourite... maybe it reminds me of a time when the kids were teeny and my laundry battles weren't quite so epic). We have also introduced some re-wear rewards in our house to help with educating the kids (see Chapter 4, Getting the Family on Board).

WASH AT 20 DEGREES

When you use the washing machine the bit that racks up your energy cost the most is heating the water. Wherever possible, I wash at 20 degrees. Modern detergents can cope with washing at low temperatures, except for laundry pods – they don't dissolve and leave a residue on your clothes. To avoid looking as if you have been the target of a particularly nasty slug ambush, I recommend using a liquid laundry detergent when washing at such low temperatures. You will save about 66% of the energy costs per wash by switching from a 40-degree to a 20-degree wash.

If you find that whites need some extra oomph, spot-treat marks and stains with spray bleach. I spray the armpits and collar of my daughter's school shirts with good old Domestos spray; for large items like sheets I add a couple of capfuls of bleach to the detergent tray. Don't do this on your best white silk number as it will literally leave you looking like Cinderella in rags before her makeover; this tip is for the hardy polycottons and cottons that, like a cockroach, can survive anything.

THE WASHING MACHINE CYCLE

How much it costs per load to wash your clothes is dependent on your machine, so I can't give you an exact answer; if you have a smart meter, play around with a few different cycles to see what uses less electricity. As a rule, most machines have an eco cycle, which heats the water and then sort of ferments your clothes in the water for a long period of time and reduces the temperature on the wash and rinse – this might be your cheapest option. After prolonged fiddling with my machine, my personal cheapest is fast and cold. I have a 14-minute, 20-degree wash on my machine that costs pennies.

DRYING

If I had a quid for every time someone asked me a question about getting laundry dry I would be living in the lap of luxury in a well-heated home by now. It's a number one bug bear. We live on a soggy little island, and even on dry days the air is filled with that very British damp and dank moisture. Meanwhile, the tumble drier has become public enemy number one with its energy-guzzling credentials. I now only use mine to finish off clothes that have been air-dried as it gets the creases out. As ironing is a thankless task that costs about 51p an hour, I'd rather spend 44p on tumble drier power and get an hour of my life back. There you go – permission to bin the iron!

"The tumble drier has become public enemy number one with its energy-guzzling credentials."

The tumble drier as last resort: Popping a dry microfibre towel in the drier with the wet washing reduces the drying time by around 30%.

Spinning around: Whatever wash cycle you have used, pop an extra fast spin on at the end to wring extra moisture out of your laundry. You can get away without this on baking hot days if you can line-dry, otherwise I would recommend squeezing every last millilitre of water out with an extra spin.

Free drying: If you are fortunate enough to have any outdoor space, check the weather forecast and hang the washing out. If it turns to rain, the drying can always be finished off over an airer indoors or in the drier for 5 to 10 minutes.

Chasing the sun: A couple of weeks ago I was on a Teams call when working from home. I glanced out of the window and it started lashing down. My blood ran cold. "Noooo!" I screamed, "I have to drop out and reschedule." Why? Well, I had spent 15 minutes diligently hanging all my washing on the line clinging to the misguided optimism that a forecast of sunshine and showers meant mostly sun and the showers wouldn't happen.

I don't think I have ever moved as quick to drag that sodden line full of washing in. If it looks glorious outside but there's a threat of rain, or you have no outdoor space, find the sunniest window in your home – it's your new best friend. You can hang clothes from the curtain rail or window surround, or pop an airer in the window. On a sunny day, you get a lovely greenhouse effect from the glass and, even if it's Baltic outside, you will be able to dry things in less than an hour. You will need to turn them around for them to dry through, but it's worth the effort for the speed and value of the process.

Air drying indoors: This sucks! When you are skimping on heating your home, heaps of wet laundry hanging around for days, filling your house with condensation is no joy. I use a heated airer, and even that's not a silver bullet. You need to lay things as flat as possible on the heated airer to get maximum bang for your buck, and it does require you to rotate the laundry so as much of it as possible is touching the bars. The bonus is the heated airer will warm the space a bit, although these airers are better covered to keep the heat trapped inside. I also run a dehumidifier when drying clothes indoors to remove moisture from the air – it helps the drying process as well as helping to stop those little black mould spots appearing on cold walls. You can pick up preloved dehumidifiers and heated airers on selling sites if you are not in a position to buy new.

If using a bog-standard airer or clothes horse, the tip is not to overlap items. If you can't fit everything on, you are better off putting some items on hangers placed on window or door frames, where the air can circulate around them, and using the clothes horse for smaller items. Directing a desk fan toward the washing will mimic the wind blowing and dry laundry quicker.

Quick-dry fabrics will forever be your friend during the long, cold, wet British winter, and maybe in spring too on an unlucky year! Switching to fleece pyjamas and loungewear will at least mean you have some clothes that dry quickly whatever the weather as they come out of the washing machine 90% dry.

BEDDING

We have three double beds in our house and nothing compares to the misery of getting three loads of bedding dry. I like to keep my house tidy, and sheets, duvets and pillowcases draped over every surface for days on end drive me to the brink of insanity. I have cried over the thankless task that is getting the bedding dry in a cold, damp house when it's been raining for 10 days solid.

But then I invested in teddy fleece bedding… game changer. It comes out of the washing machine practically dry. Not only is it toasty and warm, but it air dries in an hour or takes about 5 minutes in the drier. Mine will be my winter bedding from here on in, and I will store them with a couple of Lenor sheets in a vacuum bag when the weather gets warmer.

TOWELS

Getting wet towels dry without using a tumble drier is listed in the Oxford English Dictionary under the word "misery". They can take up to 48 hours to dry, occupy your hanging space so you get a backlog of other laundry and even then they will smell like wet dog. But I have found the solution – microfibre towels! Not the piffling little dishcloth ones, but full-sized microfibre towels with a deep pile on one side. Not only do they come out of the washing machine practically dry, but they fully air dry in an hour. They are the silver bullet of drying towels in an unheated home. I bought mine online and the whole towel bale cost less than one regular cotton bath towel. Remember when you wash them to **not** use fabric conditioner as it is kryptonite to microfibre, causing it to lose its drying superpower. Instead, use a laundry disinfectant such as Fabulosa Laundry Cleaner, which kills bacteria at 20 degrees. This product also works to eliminate some of the fustiness from regular towels when you air dry them.

TOP TAKEAWAYS
LAUNDRY ENERGY-SAVING HACKS

- Do the sniff test – can it be re-worn?
- Wear clothes more often before washing.
- Freshen worn clothes up with antibacterial fabric spray.
- Wash at 20 degrees where possible.
- Experiment to find the cheapest cycle for your machine.
- Use an extra spin at the end of your washing cycle.
- Dry outdoors where possible.
- Use sunny windows, door frames, bannisters, curtain poles and window frames to dry clothes indoors.
- Use a heated airer, but remember to lay laundry as flat as possible – and rotate!
- Use a dehumidifier.
- Use a desk fan aimed at washing to mimic wind or air flow.
- Switch winter bedding for fleece bedding.
- Switch cotton towels for microfibre towels.

SWEET SMELLING & BEAUTIFUL

We used to bathe. The kids would sit in the tub and constantly top it up with hot water, wallowing like happy little hippos for hours. Then we remodelled the bathroom four years ago and got rid of the bath completely, replacing it with a shower.

Generally speaking, showers are cheaper than baths (unless you like to sit in a cold puddle). That said, it does depend on the length of the shower. Pre-energy cost hikes my kids would take a speaker into the shower and treat it like a spa experience – now they are restricted to 5 minutes.

But worry not – I have a few simple hacks to keep you smelling sweet and looking gorgeous.

SHOWER ELSEWHERE

Lots of "green" forward-thinking workplaces have showers to encourage people to run and cycle to work rather than using cars. If you are lucky enough to still have a workplace that you actually go to and they have a shower, use it. Consider it a pay rise.

If you have a gym membership, I highly recommend taking full advantage of it by washing and drying your hair there. Not only will it mean less cleaning of your own shower, but lower home bills for water, heating and electricity for the hairdryer. It's all part of the package, so why shouldn't you?

TIME SHOWERS

This works better for younger kids, and you can get sand timers that last 5 minutes or snazzy digital timers. It's not as easy with teens, but as the light switch to our bathroom is just outside the door, if they exceed 5 minutes they are cast into darkness.

126

DO YOU NEED TO WASH YOUR HAIR?

Washing and conditioning longer hair is faffy and means that you might be in the shower a bit longer. I used to wash my hair daily but now that I work at home I wash my hair just twice a week. In between washes I use dry shampoo and tie it out of the way. It's now in much better condition, and I save on time, products and energy.

The hairdryer is the most power-hungry styling gadget, so less washes means less drying. If you wake up like me with hair that looks like Frank from *Shameless*, it's much cheaper to restyle it using straighteners or tongs.

DO YOU REALLY NEED A DAILY SHOWER?

There were numerous headlines during lockdown highlighting that when socially isolated we showered and bathed less. Do you really need to shower every day? Do you work at home all day sat in front of a computer? If so, it hardly leaves you dripping with sweat. Could you get away with the three F's (face, fanny and feet)? A camping wash in the morning might just do the trick. It will also give you an extra few minutes in bed, as well as saving you money on products, energy and water.

OTHER WORTHWHILE ENERGY-SAVING HACKS

- Adapt – we are in this for the long haul. And even if energy prices plummet, why would you want to pay more than you need to?

- Be conscious. Before the energy crisis I just didn't think about this stuff; now, I am hyper-aware about what electrical goods are running in the home, how long for and for what reason. It's forced me to get creative with solutions to run our family home as cheaply as possible.
- Continually review. Seasons change and so does the amount of energy you need. Layer on efficiency savings, and look for new ones to add to your repertoire. I have saved £50 a month on my energy use – even with the price rises.
- Think about your tolerance to cold. If it's 14 degrees outside, do you really need to heat the whole home? In previous years, you might have automatically declared it heating season when the clocks went back, but is it time for a rethink of habits?
- Introduce an energy curfew. I warn the kids the Wi-Fi is going off, then switch it off at the router. As a result, they no longer stay up late boiling kettles, making toast and gaming – all with the lights on. A lights-out curfew also reduces energy use.
- Plan meals and cooking around energy-saving gadgets
- No snacks between meals that need cooling or heating. We have gone back to three meals a day and nothing else.
- Fill a thermos and make your drinks for the day in one go.
- Make full use of free energy. Sunshine equals warmth, equals clothes drying and solar lights charging.
- Switch to LED lightbulbs.
- When you know you are going to struggle to get washing dry, use more fleece and fast-drying microfibre, bedding, clothes and towels.
- Wash clothes and bedding less and use an antibac fabric spray to freshen up.

Keep smiling. Cold is temporary, discomfort is temporary. Savings are for life!

SAVE MONEY, SAVE THE PLANET

While the main theme of this book is living thriftily to save money, consuming less energy also has a positive impact on the environment. Using less power reduces harmful pollution and toxins created by power plants as well as supporting the conservation of Earth's finite natural resources. Using less energy is a win for your bank balance and a win for the planet.

CHAPTER 6

MONEY-SAVING GROCERY SHOPPING

I used to wander around the supermarket lured in by BOGOF (buy one get one free) offers, new products and general yumminess. I shopped with my eyes and my rumbling stomach. Very often, I'd get home and feel quite ashamed that I'd only got a few proper meals in my shop and the rest was "picky bits" and niceness. This would result in me popping out midweek for a "bit of a top up". Again, I would wander into the supermarket to get a few meals and invariably come out with at least six items that I didn't need.

Another confession: in lockdown, I felt awful for my kids. Like everyone, they couldn't see their friends, and we couldn't go anywhere nice, so I became a feeder to overcompensate for the lack of joy in their lives. As life didn't hold much excitement, and about the only place I could go was the supermarket, when there I shopped to fill the fridge and cupboards with tasty delights, snacks, luxury nibbles and delicious titbits. As I was working during the day, the Deliveroo man very often delivered junk food for lunch, much to the delight of the kids; they gained weight and I spent an absolute fortune on rubbish.

Fast-forward a year, and I noticed that my £70 a week shop had become £85 a week. This then rose to £100 a week, and it was when my Aldi weekly trolley topped £137 I knew something had to change. I have managed to claw back a whopping £30 per week on my grocery shop, which over a month is a hefty amount to save, particularly with food prices increasing almost weekly. So, what did I do?

THE FOOD SHOP – PLAN, PLAN, PLAN

I am a professional planner (no, really, that *is* my day job) – I manage complex projects and programmes. In my job, I quickly learned that the only way to control outcomes (in this case how much you spend on food) is to plan ahead.

Planning is king. If you were heading on a journey from St Ives to Glasgow and you'd never driven it before, you would at least look at a map and plan your journey. If you didn't, it is highly likely that you would get lost and waste a lot of expensive fuel. It's exactly the same principle when you do your grocery shop. Your meal planner and the shopping list is your map. It means that you don't bimble out of the supermarket with a load of picky bits that you can't make a meal with. It means that you plan meals within your budget, and that you have a meal organised for every night so you are not tempted to order an emergency Chinese because there appears to be nothing for tea. I guarantee that planning ahead will save you money on your food shop and that you will waste far less food. Sticking to proper meals also means you are less inclined to snack on unhealthy treats, so it's better for your body too.

"Planning is king."

I think we can agree that all supermarkets have some products in their ranges that will be cheaper than their competitors, but unless you are flouncing around Harrods Food Hall, overall they are much of a muchness. I shopped at Aldi for years. Loyal as Old Shep, I would trudge there week after week. My closest branch is super-busy, and very often essential products that I would need would be missing from the shelves, which led to me popping back to top up. (More on the dreaded top-up shop later!) I then switched to Sainsbury's so I could use the scan and shop – that snazzy little gadget that helps you keep track of what you are spending as you go around, and also because I could weigh out my fruit and veg in the fresh grocery section.

The very first thing I did when I decided I needed to save on the food shop was start to plan the week's meals. I plan six days' evening meals and I have set a budget of £30 (six days, four people, 24 meals). Occasionally it will be higher if I need to replenish herbs, spices and seasonings. I plan the week's meals around:

- using the most energy-efficient appliances to cook
- using any leftover veg that I have in the fridge from last week's shop
- seasonings, herbs, spices that I have already
- any items that have been malingering uneaten in my freezer
- what I can batch cook and use again that week or the next week

After I have taken a mini audit of my fridge, cupboards and freezer I plan the week's meals. Now, not all meals are made equal; there are tasty, functional, keep-you-alive and reasonably healthy meals, and there are dripping in luxury meals with 15 ingredients. I recently googled affordable family meals and a celeb chef had a lovely recipe for chicken, leek and asparagus pie – I guess "affordable" is relative. If there are costly ingredients (such as asparagus out of season), then be confident to tweak existing recipes or, in this case, omit the ingredient altogether.

For years, I have weight-trained. I am 52 years old and wear the same size clothes as I did when I was 17. I do not diet. I follow a macro-balanced diet, but I am not rigid. In better times, I worked with a personal trainer and a nutritionist. Needless to say, I can no longer afford these luxuries, but my approach to eating well has stuck. I apply this mindset to meal planning for the family, as it means that I am aware of balancing carbohydrates, protein, fat and fibre in the meals that I plan for the week.

MEAL PLANNING

I use a rolling Word document to plan the week's meals, but you can do this with pen and paper too. (I suggest keeping past meal planners because you can rotate them on a cycle and it saves you a job). There are blank meal planners in the back of the book to get you started.

This is a typical week's menu for a family of four:

MONEY-SAVING GROCERY SHOPPING

Day	Meal	Ingredients for shopping	Cheapest way to cook the meal
Saturday	Sticky chicken and stir-fried noodles	Chicken thighs Soy Honey Ginger Garlic Noodles Spring onion Pepper Chinese spice	Air fryer for chicken 15 mins Wok on hob 12 mins
Sunday	Chilli con carne	Lean mince Onions Peppers Chilli Passata Tomato puree Kidney beans	Slow cooker 6 hrs
Monday	Burritos	Leftover chilli Wraps	Microwave leftovers 4 mins
Tuesday	Chicken and chorizo jambalaya	Chorizo 3 chicken breasts Onion Pepper Garlic Rice Cajun seasoning Chicken stock Tinned tomatoes	Slow cooker 6 hrs

Day	Meal	Ingredients for shopping	Cheapest way to cook the meal
Wednesday	Chicken casserole	Chicken thighs Carrots Potato Stock Leek Onion Pearl barley	Slow cooker 6 hrs
Thursday	Chilli pesto pasta	Pasta (quick cook) Chilli pesto Onion Pepper Bacon Garlic bread	Hob 4 mins Air fryer for garlic bread 8 mins
Friday	Ham and veggie bake	Frozen cauliflower Flour Milk Cheese Broccoli Ham Onion	Slow cooker 5 hrs

As you can see, I have planned meals that can be cooked using the slow cooker where possible as it's a far cheaper option than using the hob or the oven in terms of energy use. I also use my air fryer and George Foreman health grill as they are also much cheaper than using the main oven. If you are buying an air fryer for the first time, I would recommend looking for one with a number of shelves or sufficient capacity to be able to cook multiple things in. There is no point cooking chips in the air fryer and having no space for the chicken to go with it and having to use an additional appliance. Try and plan meals that you can cook using a single energy source where possible.

"Try and plan meals that you can cook using a single energy source where possible."

HEIDI'S HINTS
BATCH COOKING

In a slow cooker you can use two Maggi bags or slow cooker bags to cook two portions of different food at the same time, saving effort and energy; this is great for veggie and non-veggie options too. Just make sure that you get rid of a lot of the air from the bags before sealing with a bag tie.

To make my menu for the week, I populate the left-hand column with the meal and pop the ingredients on the right. For meal ideas I use Google, ask my mum and her friends what they used to cook on a budget, think back to school home economics classes in the frugal early 1980s, google wartime meals and adapt modern meals. I ask friends for their go-to dinner when they are cash-strapped. I think about what can be batch cooked and how I can make meat stretch further. And I always stick religiously to my budget.

Below is a seven-day meal plan, and you can see that I have included a vegetarian dish. Having a meatless night can reduce your food bill dramatically over the month.

HEIDI'S HINTS
SPEEDY PASTA

I use quick cook pasta as it cooks in just four minutes. In fact, you can even just add hot water and leave it to sort itself out if you want to be a complete miser.

Day	Meal	Ingredients for shopping	Cheapest way to cook the meal
Saturday	Chicken kofta	Heck mince Spring onion Harissa Pitta Green salad	Health grill 10 mins
Sunday	Chicken casserole	Chicken Leftover carrots Leftover onions Parsnip Leftover spuds Stock (have already)	Slow cooker 6 hrs

Day	Meal	Ingredients for shopping	Cheapest way to cook the meal
Monday	Dirty Dogs	Hot dogs Jalapenos Leftover potatoes Onions (have already) Cheese (have already)	Pan fry 10 mins
Tuesday	Thai sticky stir fry	Chicken Broccoli Spring onion Beans Rice Sweet chilli	Stir Fry 10 mins
Wednesday	Mediterranean chicken	Chicken Lemon (have already) Garlic, oregano, smoked paprika, honey, cumin (have already) Rice Green salad	Health grill chicken 10 mins Microwave rice 2 mins
Thursday	Pasta with ham	Spaghetti (have already) Ham Chilli pesto	Hob 4 mins
Friday	Cheese & potato pie	Frozen mash (defrost) Onion (have already) Leek Milk (have already) Mustard (have already) Cheese (have already) Beans	Air fryer 20 mins

"The key to success is sticking to your plan."

For some reason, as mum, it seems to be my job to understand what every other bugger in the house wants for tea. If you find winners on your weekly planner, I would suggest developing a rotating plan for the month with tried and tested favourites as it will save you a lot of planning time and a lot of irritation when your little darlings turn their nose up at your culinary delights.

The key to success is sticking to your plan; if this means batch cooking to save you a night of food prep then plan for this. For example, the Sunday night chilli found on the first menu plan is repurposed to make easy-peasy burritos on Monday night – all you need to do is top the chilli with some cheese in a wrap and blast in the microwave. Work meals around your schedule: on evenings when you are likely to be late home or rushing out, make sure you have a leftovers meal planned.

THE SHOPPING LIST

This is the list you schlep around the supermarket with. I list all the ingredients that I need to make the meals for the week and put a note next to what I have got in the house already after checking the fridge, freezer and cupboards. This means I use everything up in the fridge and avoid unnecessary purchases (especially important for herbs and spices that I don't use very often). The key is to **stick to the list** – you will be surprised at how much cheaper your food shop is. It takes me about 20 minutes to plan the meals and the shopping list each week, but this 20 minutes saves me at least £30.

MONEY-SAVING GROCERY SHOPPING

Protein – meat, fish, eggs & cheese (Total cost = £15.21)	
Mince Beef	£4.29
Chicken thighs x 2 packs	£5.18
Chicken	Have 3 x breasts in freezer
Ham	£2.25
Bacon	£1.49
Chorizo	£2
Cheese	Have already
Vegetables (Total cost = £5.59)	
Red onion x 2	30p
Onions x 4	80p
Chilli	£1
Broccoli	40p
Spring onion	49p
Peppers	£1
Garlic	20p
5 carrots	40p
2 large potatoes	55p
1 leek	45p
Frozen cauliflower	Have already
Carbohydrates (Total cost = £ 4.90)	
Pasta	85p
Noodles	£1
Wraps	£1.20
Rice	70p
Garlic bread x 2	70p
Kidney beans	45p

Seasonings & sauces, etc. (Total cost = £2.60)	
Tomato puree	50p
Passata	Have already
Lentils	Have already
Chinese five spice	Have already
Tinned tomatoes	50p
Honey	Have already
Soy sauce	Have already
Cajun seasoning	Have already
Stock	£1
Pesto	£1.10

Total cost for week = £28.30 for six days' evening meals for four people, so 24 meals costing an average of £4.71 a day or £1.17 per meal.

The reason I add prices to my shopping list is that I check online first. The supermarkets are savvy and they don't put the cheapest version of things at eye level (unless it's a loss leader promotion). Very often, the cheapest version will be an import in the world food section or a brand you don't recognise. A quick look online for the cheapest version of what I am looking for familiarises me with the packaging making hunting it down on the supermarket shelves far easier.

THE "EVERYTHING ELSE LIST" (AKA AVOID THE TOP-UP SHOP!)

Once I have planned and listed ingredients required for the week's dinners, I jot down everything else that we need including drinks, milk, cereal and other basics like frozen chips. I know that you will be thinking I am insane for buying everything in one place, but hear me out. Yes, I could nip to B&M for cleaning stuff, and Poundland for toiletries and Aldi for sauces. There is a reason that I get my shopping in one place: the top-up shop is the enemy.

Being brutally honest, who can pop into a discount shop and not get distracted? Have you ever gone to Poundland for deodorant and come out with a bag of tat and found yourself £20 lighter? Have you ever gone to B&M for fabric softener and tin foil and come out with a set of mugs, a bathmat, some tea lights and a Toblerone? There is nothing wrong with these discount stores – the issue is me. And if you are in any way similar and tempted by an impulse purchase, the only way to avoid leaking money in your budget is to avoid the top-up shop. Get everything in one place and look for the bargains in the one supermarket. Once the groceries for the week have gone, they have gone. No topping up, no replacing the treats that the kids have munched through on day one. This will save you time, fuel and money. It also means on the last day before shopping day your fridge and cupboards will feel empty – which is a good thing. It prevents food waste, as it makes you use everything that you already have. My kids have gone from having a constantly topped-up fridge to learning to eke the good stuff out. To be honest, as I have stopped buying snacks, the kids have consequently stopped hanging around the fridge snuffling for snackage, which in itself is a blessing. I have a matte black fridge and the greasy finger marks of my little goblins used to drive me insane, and now the grubby paw prints have vanished – bliss.

"I have saved a bomb on my food shop by cutting all the snacks."

SNACKS

Not so long ago, we had a whole crisp drawer in our kitchen, a treat box, a biscuit box and cereal bars that could be eaten as snacks at any time. Then... I just stopped buying the snacks. Snacks in our house are now an orange, an apple, toast or a biscuit. If kids ask what have you got to eat, offer them an apple. If they say no, they clearly aren't hungry. I have saved a bomb on my food shop by cutting all the snacks.

Equally with fresh juices, I have replaced these with cordial or good old-fashioned water. The kids have both lost some of their lockdown snack weight gain and are a healthy weight. They also tend to eat all their proper meals, meaning less food waste.

AN EVEN TIGHTER BUDGET

Sometimes life serves you a whole jar of lemons – whether it be the loss of a job or a partner, a huge bill or fine, or an unexpected cost – and you can be left pulling in your belt so hard it feels that you can't breathe. My most recent change in fortune has been the loss of my partner and his contribution to running a home. In order to make my single salary stretch, I have had to bring out the big guns and flex how I grocery shop again. Food prices continue to soar and my income seems to continue to dwindle.

I knew I needed a new tactic to be able to feed me, two kids and three cats for the month and Sainsbury's and Aldi felt like a luxury. I went back to the drawing board and looked for opportunities to feed us all for less and came up with a solution that worked.

The monthly plan! It involves compromising on using fresh ingredients, and bulk-buying frozen meat and veg instead. And rather than making all meals from scratch I included some budget frozen pizza and pies that were on offer, where the raw ingredients would have cost more than their frozen alternatives. Most of all it involves dropping any snobbery about using budget frozen food supermarkets like Farmfoods, Iceland or Heron Foods.

The price per kilo for basics like chicken varies enormously between supermarkets selling fresh meat and budget frozen food stores. I have found it to be about 20% cheaper buying the frozen version. There are also non-frozen bargains worth keeping an eye out for: cooking sauces, pasta and noodles can often be almost 50% cheaper in the budget stores.

In a busy house, where kids come and go, make last-minute plans and often eat at friends, I also found I was lovingly prepping meals that would go to waste. There is far less waste with using frozen food – after all you only take what you need from the freezer and the rest can be used later, unlike using exclusively fresh meat and veg that can spoil if not used or caught in time to freeze.

Nowadays, I shop monthly for the core frozen ingredients, and then only shop weekly for fresh veg, bread, milk and other basics. Using this method, I have reduced the monthly food spend down to £65 on frozen food (which makes up the basis for evening meals) and a £40 weekly shop. That is a huge 30% reduction on what we were spending previously. I make sure that we have a jacket spud night, which keeps costs down, and also a pasta night every week as pasta with a jar of pesto, garlic and some frozen spinach is a winner in our house (I sometimes add a few rashers of bacon if I am feeling flush). Frozen chicken and vegetables are just as nutritious as fresh, and I try to replicate meals that I would make using fresh ingredients using the much cheaper frozen alternatives. This method of shopping and cooking on a budget relies on having three square meals a day: a cereal breakfast, a packed lunch and an evening meal. Snacks between meals are out, as are treats. Unsurprisingly, since eliminating all snacks my body fat percentage has also dropped by 4%, which is no mean feat for a menopausal momma far past her prime.

Making a monthly plan isn't as onerous as it first sounds. I do a two-week plan and then rotate it; I get the kids involved in planning so I only buy stuff that they will eat, as I cannot afford to waste food and I want them to enjoy their evening meals. Below is my typical plan and shopping list for the month. Rotating the plan also means that where I use half a bag of crispy chicken for one meal, I can make sure that I use the whole bag before I need to shop again, and I make the most of everything I have in the freezer.

Week One						
Pasta Night	Shredded crispy chicken in sweet chilli with rice	Jacket potato cheese and beans	Spaghetti Bolognese	Chilli and rice	Chicken curry and rice	Sausage roast
Week Two						
Pasta Night	Chicken chow mein	Jacket potato, tuna and salad	Chicken fajitas and fries	Pizza, chips and salad	Chicken & broccoli stir fry	Pie, mash and veg

Week Three						
sta ght	Shredded crispy chicken in sweet chilli with rice	Jacket potato cheese and beans	Spaghetti Bolognese	Chilli and rice	Chicken curry and rice	Sausage roast
Week Four						
sta ght	Chicken chow mein	Jacket potato tuna and salad	Chicken fajitas and fries	Pizza, chips and salad	Chicken and broccoli stir fry	Pie, mash and veg

From my meal plan, I then work out a monthly shopping list so
I do not get *too* distracted when shopping.

Shopping list

2 large bags of pasta

Pesto x 4 jars

1 x extra-large bag of shredded
chicken

Sweet chilli sauce

4 bags of frozen chicken breasts

Bag of large potatoes

Tuna x 4 cans

Beans x 4 cans

Large bag of beef mince

Passata x 2

Tomato puree x 2

Rice

Spaghetti

2 bags frozen chips

Frozen sausages

Frozen Mash x 2

Pizza x 2

Stir fry veg

Broccoli

Green Beans

Spinach

Pies x 8

I now use frozen veg as it reduces waste and is affordable and just as healthy. To eke out the frozen meat, I make sure that I add plenty of vegetables to the recipes to bulk out meals. By adding handfuls of much cheaper frozen veg to a stir fry means that I can scrimp on the pricier chicken and make it last the month. By using sausages (rather than a joint of meat) to make a roast, I can cut the costs of a Sunday lunch. Using shredded chicken strips, peppers and onions mixed in sweet chilli sauce makes a convincing crispy shredded chicken fake-away.

"Frozen veg reduces waste and is affordable and just as healthy."

HEIDI'S HINTS
FROZEN FOOD

When cooking frozen food, defrost it in the fridge overnight; it will cook just as well when defrosted and halve your energy costs. The chilled food defrosting in your fridge will also cool the fridge and reduce running costs.

I also make sure that I take advantage of any discount coupons or offers by signing up online. Both Iceland and Farmfoods offer discounts, and Iceland even deliver straight to your door for free!

PACKED LUNCHES

The quality and value of school dinners varies. The canteen at my kids' secondary school is privately run and not subsidised.

Potato wedges will set you back £1.80, a bottle of Radnor Splash (basically flavoured water) a lofty £2. I have two school-age kids, and they would need £4 a day each to eat in the canteen (they are not allowed off the school grounds). So that's a combined total of £40 a week. Get out of town! There is noooo way I am wasting my money on this when I could buy 20 bags of potato wedges for that. Instead, they have:

- bagel (gets less smushed up in a bag than bread) with cream cheese and or sliced cheese and lettuce
- crisps from a multipack (supermarket own and stashed so they can't find them between meals)
- a cereal bar
- a sausage roll
- a bottle of water
- an apple.

This costs me £13.89 a week in total for both children. I go for cheese rather than cooked meats, as kids don't get to use a fridge for their packed lunch so it's not too awful at room temperature. I can foil wrap the sausage rolls and bagels (these tend to keep better in the fridge than sliced bread) on Sunday for the whole week so they can grab and go every day.

ADULT PACKED LUNCHES

Cheese is a staple and used to schuzz up pasta dishes at dinner, so cheese sandwiches are generally on the menu. I focus on buying products that you can use again during the week. If you are cooking a pasta dish for the week, make sure that you cook too much. Pasta, tuna and sweetcorn is a good budget lunch. If you are boiling pasta, throw some eggs in the boiling water to make an egg salad or sandwich. Don't waste the opportunity to prepare your packed lunch food while you are using energy to cook your evening meal. If you are lucky enough to be able to use a microwave at work, leftovers from the evening before work well as a packed lunch.

We all know the feeling of getting in from work shattered, when you just can't face getting ready for the next day. It can feel like you are on a treadmill – working, prepping for work and sleeping – bear in mind that cheese sandwiches can be made up for the week and wrapped in foil in the fridge. Egg salad is good for three days. Cold meats are good for three days. Prepping in advance will help you to avoid shelling out for overpriced shop and café lunches.

If you are fed up of chomping through dry stale sandwiches at the end of the week I would highly recommend keeping sliced bread in the fridge; this will prevent it going mouldy and keep it fresh for up to two weeks.

Whatever you plan for lunches, make sure that you put your ingredients on your shopping list and, as ever, **stick to the list**.

CHEAP & FREE FOOD

There's no shame in asking for help if you really need it.

A House of Commons Library report states that the Independent Food Aid Network (IFAN) surveyed food banks within their network between April to August 2022, and 90% of the food banks in their network saw a rise in demand, with over half of them finding that 25% or more of the people they supported hadn't used their services before.

There are also signs that a wider range of the population is resorting to using food banks: social workers, public sector workers, teachers and people in employment more generally.

Food banks provide emergency three-day food parcels. It tends to be non-perishable goods – typically canned and dried food – so it's not going to be easy to make a meal with; but that combined with some fresh food from Olio (the app that passes on unwanted food) and you may just be able to scratch a meal together.

Olio

I love Olio. It's a free app that connects communities and local businesses, ensuring that surplus food is shared instead of being thrown away (and there are food and non-food sections, too). I had a quick glance while I was typing away at this chapter, and I could have collected:

- celery
- a loaf of bread
- pastries from Tesco Bakery
- green beans
- chicken & bacon salad
- smoked ham
- cucumber & tomatoes
- malt loaf

I think you get the idea – it's totally random. The food will be nearing its expiry date, but if you've managed to pick up some veggies, once you cook them or use them in a meal you can get an extra few days out of them. You might need to get creative, but could you make celery and ham soup? Yes, I think you could! Would the bread be okay for toast or bread pudding? Abso-bloody-lutely. You might need to get a bit "Ready Steady Cook", but with some imagination you really can bolster your food budget with some Olio goodies (and help to eliminate food waste at the same time).

OLIO non-food

Olio also has a non-food section where you can pick up toiletries, sanitary products, clothes, toys, games and furniture. My daughter was complaining that she needed a new bikini in the height of summer; I looked on Olio and found a brand-new bikini with the tags still on less than 0.5 miles away. Within half an hour I'd collected it and my daughter had got the bikini she was looking for at no cost. I also regularly give away items on Olio, from cushions and kids games to books. It keeps everything circular.

TOO GOOD TO GO

This is a brilliant app that is designed to curb food waste by connecting local retailers and communities. The food isn't free, but it's heavily discounted, and there are some great deals to be had. I have personally tried bags from Starbucks, Greggs, Costa and YO! Sushi. The food has generally got to be eaten on the day that you pick it up as its stuff that the cafés or shops haven't sold that day. I have eked it out an extra day and used a Too Good to Go bag for a beach snack for the kids the next day. The best value one I have had was a Greggs bag for £2.49. Splitting a bag with a friend would make it even better value. I was not that impressed with the Starbucks and Costa bags, but it really is the luck of the draw what you end up with.

SUPERMARKET YELLOW STICKERS

Supermarkets work their yellow sticker magic at different times. There are, however, some great times when you are almost guaranteed to grab some bargains. Christmas Eve is one of these. Supermarkets generally close Xmas Day and Boxing Day, so it's worth popping in a few hours before they close to purchase knocked-down meat and other fresh stuff that can be frozen. You can prep and freeze most veggies, and you can make smoothies and freeze them too. The same goes for the Saturday afternoon before Easter Sunday. Beware of buying items that aren't useful just because they have a yellow sticker. It's easy to get lured in by a bargain, but if it's no use whatsoever it's not a bargain. Meat is always a good buy. I am also a fan of a damaged can sticker and a deli counter deal – the cooked food section is brilliant as they only have so long to sell hot food. I have bagged a whole chicken for £1.16 from Morrisons' hot food counter, along with pies for 9p. I stockpile if I get the opportunity, by letting them cool and freeze them.

COMMUNITY GROUPS

I am a massive fan of Facebook Marketplace for finding second-hand tat, and there are also lots of local community groups on Facebook where people offer help (and you can reach out for help if you need it too). We have a local Don't Dump It website, where a lovely lady cooks extra Sunday roast every week and offers dinners. It is always worth a call out on a social media post if you find yourself in dire straits, as there are some good eggs out there willing to help out. There is no shame in asking for help when you need it. I recently collected 52 pouches of cat food for free because a local cat decided that top brand Sheba no longer suited their delicate palate. Within 10 minutes of replying to the giveaway post on the group, I had £20 worth of cat meat for free.

TOP TAKEAWAYS
MONEY-SAVING
GROCERY SHOPPING

- Always plan your meals ahead.
- Always audit your fridge, freezer and cupboards before going shopping, and plan meals that use leftovers and things you have already.
- Take a shopping list – and stick to it.
- Avoid top-up shops; buy enough on your shopping trip to not have to revisit the supermarket until the next week.
- Use lentils mixed with mince: it's added protein and makes the meat go further. When making a chilli, I add extra kidney beans to bulk it out.
- Batch cook chicken, onions and peppers and freeze. This is a great base for fajitas, curries and stir fries.
- Batch cook minced beef and onions; one lot of cooking saves energy and is a base for a cottage pie, minced beef and onion pie, spag bol, chilli, burritos and enchiladas.

- Adapt complicated recipes with multiple ingredients to fit your budget, making cheaper compromises where you can.
- Use extra cheap veggies, like onions, to bulk meals out.
- Cut chicken breasts into thinner fillets so that they cook quicker and you can control child portions more easily.
- Instead of buying burgers, use chicken, turkey or beef mince and make your own – you get double the bang for your buck.
- Weigh loose fruit and vegetables rather than buying prepacked – and only buy what you need (always check the unit price of the bagged veg and if the loose is cheaper buy that). Sometimes the bagged wonky veg is cheaper, so check first.
- When I buy broccoli I don't weigh the stem – I snap it off as I don't want to buy that bit.
- Snap off the bit of ginger you need for a recipe – you don't need a whole stem.
- Use quick cook pasta.
- Bring rice to the boil, cover pan, switch off the hob and leave it – it will continue to cook for free.
- Use Idahoan mash (today's Smash) or frozen mash (defrosted) – both are quicker, easier and cheaper (if you take off the energy costs of boiling spuds so that they are soft enough to mash).
- Frozen ingredients are cheaper, and you get more for your money. I do try to prep a couple of days at a time, but have one pizza night a week which allows for an emergency "I can't be arsed to cook, lazy night", and stops me calling for a takeaway. (Tip... cut the pizza in half to fit in the air fryer.)

- Ignore best before dates: sniff it; if it smells okay then eat it. Are there slimy bits on your veg? Cut them off and eat the rest.
- Veg on the turn? Don't throw it: soup it or freeze it (freezing goes for garlic, herbs and ginger too).
- Don't waste anything. If you've cooked a whole chicken, boil the carcass overnight on the lowest slow cooker setting, sieve off the golden nectar and use it as a fabulous, tasty soup base. You can portion it up and pop it in the freezer.
- Defrost any frozen food before cooking – it then cooks in a third of the time, saving you energy.
- Store sliced bread in the fridge to keep it fresh for up to two weeks.

CHAPTER 7

KEEP WARM ON
A SHOESTRING

It's December 2022. I am writing this chapter in a house that was built in 1855. I am wearing thermals, a woolly balaclava, two pairs of socks and multiple layers. You might have guessed – I do not have the heating on. As an experiment a few months ago, I put my heating on for two hours one Saturday evening, and it cost £7. This coupled with daily electricity costs of around £7 makes it an unaffordable daily total for my family. I promptly switched the heating off and resigned myself to the fact that we would revert back to our "heat the person, not the room" tactics.

It's not my first time at this rodeo. Back in October 2019, we had work done to the house to remedy a falling-down kitchen extension. The back wall to the house was removed and we had a large piece of plastic sheeting between us and the elements. We had no boiler, no hot water and no heating. The family lived in one room, showered at the gym and at friends', and we snuggled under blankets to keep warm. The work was completed in February 2020 (before lockdown thank goodness!), and we survived. No one in the family got ill or was psychologically damaged by it.

BRAVING THE ELEMENTS

I am not passively accepting this, frankly often uncomfortable, situation, but there is only so much within my control that I can do right now. I could be angry, I could feel sorry for myself, I could complain. None of these things will help. Instead, I am adapting. There is no right or wrong to my decision to keep the heating off, but it does feel like we are in this for the long haul; and even beyond an energy crisis, I am all in for spending less on energy and doing my bit to reduce my carbon footprint too. During a particularly cold week of sub-zero temperatures, the sun miraculously made an appearance one afternoon. I seized the moment by quickly rearranging the furniture, pulled a chair up to the window and enjoyed the free warmth pouring in through the sunny window.

Despite feeling cold, there is always something to be grateful for. I always try to find a positive in the worst situations, so I have head space to think of practical things I can do to come through and out the other side. I have found the following positives from not using central heating.

- My skin and hair are better. In mid-winter I usually resemble a frazzled prune.
- I have had less head colds and sniffles.
- My house plants haven't shrivelled up and died.
- My tolerance for cold has increased, and rather than automatically popping the heating on when it feels a bit nippy, I rarely feel cold enough to justify using any heating.

The UK Health Security Agency recommend heating your home to at least 18 degrees. If you are sick, elderly or disabled, or have a very young child in your home you are going to need to live somewhere that isn't like a Siberian wilderness. Of course, this is great if you can afford it – but what do you do if you simply can't?

"I always try to find a positive in the worst situations."

This chapter offers tips to keep warm while spending as little as possible. This is about picking and choosing what works best for you and your family.

Moisture hacks

What is it about the word "moist" that everyone hates? Who knows? But I'm afraid we need to talk about damp and moisture. Living in an unheated house, trying to air-dry laundry can leave your house feeling damp and also risks black mould appearing. Even in a really well insulated home, the advice for combatting damp and keeping warm is tricky as you need ventilation and airflow to prevent moisture building up. I have adapted to living in an unheated house by using these hacks.

- Run the dehumidifier overnight.
- Hang wardrobe damp traps over window levers.
- Place bowls of salt on windowsills to absorb moisture.
- Wipe off condensation from windows every morning.
- Open blinds and curtains.
- If it's not perishingly cold outside, open the windows for an hour.
- Treat black spots that appear on cold walls with white vinegar in a spray bottle: leave for an hour and wipe off; HG Mould Spray is a professional cleaner that will kill the spores.

FINANCIAL HELP

If you meet certain criteria you may be able to seek support with energy bills through grants and schemes. These are subject to change, so the best place to find out what current help is available is the Government's website, gov.uk (search "Help for Households"). If you find it hard to navigate or need someone to advocate or signpost for you I would recommend Citizens Advice, Age UK or your Local Authority. That said, the support available is limited, and even with support you are unlikely to be able to heat your home in the way you used to.

MIDDLE EARNERS

I am writing this from a privileged place – and also not such a privileged place. I consider myself lucky to be in full-time employment; I have two reasonably low-maintenance teenage kids that really don't require much from me apart from feeding, watering and Wi-Fi. As a family, we do not qualify for any additional support, benefits or grants toward the cost of living (apart from the October to March Energy Bill Support Scheme that was available to all UK households). Our family budget is squeezed and we juggle priorities, but we have a roof over our heads and food in the fridge. We did not, however, enjoy the luxury of central heating during what seemed to be a very long winter.

We are not alone. The aspirational middle earners with their mortgages, annual holidays and disposable income are seeing that disposable income erode as it is chipped away at by the rising cost of... everything. In a salaried job there is often very little opportunity to work overtime to increase income, so for us the main way to maintain a standard of living is to cut back on outgoings, including heating costs.

KEEPING WARM FOR LESS

LAYERS

Yup, energy crisis chic is a thing. I regularly rock up on Teams calls for work in a balaclava, two jumpers, layered thermals, two pairs of socks and a coat. It's common sense, but covering up in multiple layers really does trap the heat in. And, if you are sat at a keyboard all day, fingerless gloves are a must.

HATS

There are lots of myths related to how much heat you can lose from an uncovered head. The fable that you can lose 45% of your body heat through your head is believed to have come from a 1950s US Army Field Manual. It is, in fact, bunkum – unless you have a disproportionally and exceptionally large head. In actual fact, heat loss is related to surface area, and your head accounts for approximately 10% of your overall body surface area. Still, retaining an extra 10% heat is worth popping a beanie on or pulling your hood up for, whether you're indoors or outdoors.

FINGERLESS GLOVES

The very worst part of being cold at home is frozen fingers. This is brutal if you work at home on a laptop all day – you can feel the gradual clawing of your hands, and by midday your hands are rendered useless as atrophy sets in. Fingerless gloves or mittens to cover the majority of the hands are a must, and they still allow for typing, tea making and phone scrolling.

FLEECE

Oodies, snoodies, fleecy hoodies – those ridiculous-looking, knee-length, hooded fleecy things are an essential. Buy one in the biggest size you can to wear over your multiple layers. You will not win any style awards but, by God, you will not want to take it off either. I have been known to sneak out on errands with mine concealed under my puffer coat when temperatures drop to Siberian levels. When your morning alarm goes off, drag your snoodie into bed with you and warm it up while you snooze. Do not leave the comfort of your bed without fleecing up. It's a total game changer – and you will feel sad when you take it off. If you don't have one already, make sure you buy one in the sales when the weather gets warmer. Always buy out of season to bag a bargain.

"Don't underestimate the good old-fashioned hot water bottle."

ANALOGUE HEATING

Don't underestimate the good old-fashioned hot water bottle; make sure it's not older than god's dog though or you will end up with scorched legs coated in hot rubber. The hot water bottle is great to warm up hands that have started to claw in the cold. I like to pop mine inside my hoodie, between layers, and it keeps me warm for a few hours.

CANDLES

A few lit candles really do take the chilly edge off a room if you keep the door closed. It goes without saying not to put them near anything flammable. I have seen lots of videos on TikTok suggesting that you make heaters with candles and terracotta pots – I have also seen videos from the Fire Service saying not to. As cold as it is, I don't actually want to burn the house down, so I have avoided these. I stock up with candles from The Range and Primark. Needless to say, burning through Jo Malone and Diptyque candles to keep warm isn't going to be very cost effective.

ACTIVITY

Once an hour, I get up and do 50 star jumps. God knows what the window cleaner thinks of me, but it elevates my heart rate and my temperature and keeps me warm for a good 20 minutes. Moving helps. If you haven't got a star jump in you, get the vacuum out for an intensive hoovering sesh – kill two birds, and all that.

GO OUTSIDE

I see you – shoulders hunched, swaddled in blankets, teeth chattering, trying to contemplate another day in the cold wasteland that is your house. As counterintuitive as it seems, step outside, have a quick brisk walk. When it's freezing outside, it will feel more comfortable in your house when you come back indoors.

STAY IN ONE ROOM

For the first time in eons, my son sat next to me on the sofa and we snuggled up under the heated blanket. My daughter was sat next to her dad also sharing a blanket. My heart was full – they think we are tragic and don't generally want to grace us middle-aged saddos with their youthful presence for more than half an hour. The body heat from all of us in the same room made it feel cosy, and I felt like I was living in a Hallmark family movie.

PUBLIC SPACES

Lockdowns made remote working the new norm for lots of us, and for many the office no longer exists or is 200 miles away. Your laptop and screen don't use much energy, but when it's so cold at home that you can't feel your face, it proves a long day at the home office. Depending on what your work requires, you can seek a warm sanctuary elsewhere. I have tested Pret A Manger, Wetherspoon's and the local library. 'Spoons tops the list because of the bottomless coffee, so it's great for report writing and desk-based work; however, it's not going to work if you are going to breach confidentiality having customer conversations. Even if it's just for the odd reprieve or if your pre-paid meter is out of credit, it's always an option to work somewhere warm for a few hours.

If you are clinging on to your monthly gym membership and justifying it with the free shower, spend a few hours in the evening in the gym. Not only is it good for your mental and physical health, it will warm you up more than sitting in front of the TV.

SHARE THE BURDEN

In the middle of an Arctic blast, you may feel compelled to have the central heating on. There are a few times in the year when we experience extreme cold weather, and it becomes all that anyone talks about. The weather will be all over the news and severe weather warnings issued. These are the times when you will need to spend precious pennies on heating. If all you do in the evening is eat dinner and slump on the sofa in front of Netflix, why not share the heating burden with friends or family by taking it in turns to heat your homes and watch TV together. Rather than eating and heating separate homes, buddy up and alternate evenings. It will save all of you money, and you get to stay cosy and warm until the cold snap has eased.

Get your hustle on

Faced with brutally cold temperatures last winter, I decided to get my hustle on. Where could I make some quick cash to balance out the heating costs? I realised I hadn't used my car for two weeks so had saved £20 on running costs; and I remembered an old air fryer sitting unloved in my kitchen cupboard – I sold it on Facebook Marketplace for £40.

I logged on to my energy provider app and paid the extra £60 into my account. Now I had about 16 hours' worth of heating paid for, ready for when the cold became unbearable, or as a treat over Christmas. Clearing out and selling clutter is a great way to make some extra cash, especially before Christmas when new clutter will make its way into your home.

GADGETS & GIZMOS TO KEEP YOU WARM

ELECTRIC BLANKETS

In winter, I can spend 16 hours of my day shuffling around like a fleece-clad Michelin Man. There are, however, a sweet eight hours when I am so warm and toasty that I forget that it's cold. An electric underblanket is the number one thing to invest in. Mine makes me feel like a baby marsupial crawling into its mama's cosy pouch. Getting into a bed with fleece bedding *and* an electric blanket is pure joy. It may not make the covers of an interiors magazine in terms of style, but for warmth and comfort that costs a mere 1p an hour to run, it is a great solution. Sleep with it on the minimum setting to keep you toasty and happy all night. Forget far-flung shores, my cosy bed is my favourite place in the world. If you don't have an electric blanket already, it's another one of those very seasonal things that is cheaper if you buy it in summer. I guarantee that you, too, will become an electric blanket evangelist.

"An electric underblanket is the number one thing to invest in."

Early to bed

How do you *really* spend your midweek evenings? We all like to pretend that we have dazzling, exciting lives, but if you are anything like my family, the teens retire to their rooms and spend the night chatting on WhatsApp to people that they have been with all day, while I settle down to watch TV with my phone in my hand. In this scenario, you may as well take the laptop or tablet to bed with you, switch the electric blanket on and enjoy the warmth. When all else fails, take your lead from hedgehogs and hibernate.

HEATED THROWS

Very much like a portable electric blanket that goes over you, they cost a few pence per hour to run and are lovely and cosy. I bought mine when it was a sizzling 32 degrees outside in August and paid £12.99. At the time of writing, in deepest winter, they are now £70. The cat that's not usually bothered whether you're around or not will all of a sudden want to sit on your lap, which is another bonus. The throws are thankfully washable, and really do make a huge difference to your quality of life when it's cold.

PLUG-IN HEATERS

I have decided that we are better off adapting to the cold than using plug-in heaters as its robbing Peter to pay Paul. They are expensive to run (but cheaper than central heating); they only heat one room and the heat quickly dissipates – although you can run a dehumidifier in the room at the same time which will help circulate the warm air, but then you are adding another load to your electric usage. If needs must, I have found the halogen heaters to be the cheapest option, and not as drying or noisy.

> ## "When all else fails, take your lead from hedgehogs and hibernate."

You can buy teeny heaters that run at 500W that are a lot cheaper to run; but unless you are in a small box room it will take a good 30 minutes to make any difference to the temperature in the room.

The only time I use the plug-in heater is to get the kids up and dressed for school. I give them 5 minutes of heater time each. It's the one thing I have found that drags reluctant teens out of bed. I also crank up the electric blanket heat setting before they wake up as this boils them in their beds and they are glad to escape the stifling heat of an electric blanket at full pelt!

CALOR GAS HEATERS

I spent December through to March coveting a Calor gas heater, but the prices were prohibitively high, inflated by a combination of inflated energy costs and a long cold winter. Instead, I purchased one in May, during a particularly hot week – when the temperature rises, the demand for anything heating related drops. Ever the Girl Guide, I am now better prepared for next winter. I will make sure it uses the same gas canister as the barbecue, so if there is any left it will get used.

OTHER GADGETS

There are all sorts of gadgets out there designed to warm you up: USB heated loo seats, heated computer mice, microwavable hand warmers. But consider how much you need them before parting with cash.

The sensible stuff

- Seal off drafts. Insulate your doors and windows with adhesive strips, and use draft excluders and curtains.
- Keep doors closed to keep any heat in.
- If you are going to use central heating:
  - experiment with your smart meter to gauge cost
  - set the thermostat to 18 degrees
  - turn down or off radiators in any rooms you don't use
  - make sure radiators are bled
  - make sure your thermostat is in the warmest place in the house – ideally where you all spend the most time; if you

keep the thermostat in the coldest far-flung corner of your house you will be burning through fivers

o have your boiler serviced annually, and ask your boiler technician for advice on how to make sure you are getting the most bang for your buck from the boiler

HEAT SOURCE COSTS

The table below is a sliding scale from the lowest to highest heat source costs based on April 2023 Energy Price Guarantee unit costs. You can calculate the most up-to-date costs using the Sust-It energy calculator online, but the scale below will remain indicative. I have not included fossil fuel heat sources, such as log burners and open fires, as the cost of coal and wood is so fluid it would be impossible to capture accurately. Note, a single heater will only warm one space compared to central heating that will warm the whole home. Armed with this knowledge, you can make calculated decisions that fit with your needs, lifestyle and budget.

Heat Source	Wattage	Cost per hour
Extra clothes	0	£0
Snoodie	0	£0
Hot water bottle	0	5p to boil kettle
Heated public spaces (e.g. pub, local library, museum, art gallery)	0	from £0
Heated throw	85W	0.5p
Electric underblanket	200W	1p
Dehumidifier	400W	14p

Heat Source	Wattage	Cost per hour
Mini fan heater	500W	17p
Halogen heater	1000W	34p
Oil filled radiator	1500W	51p
Fan heater	3000W	£1.02
Gas central heating	24kW	£2.40

HEIDI'S HINTS
FREE WATER

Use the water collected in the dehumidifier to water plants or flush the loo.

TOP TAKEAWAYS
KEEP WARM ON A SHOESTRING

Shuffling around swearing and saying, "This is horrible,"
doesn't help. These things will:

- Check to see if you are available for any grants or support.
- Buy things to keep you warm, like heated blankets, electric blankets, hot water bottles and fleecy oodies; and buy out of season to bag a bargain.
- An electric blanket is the best thing since sliced bread.
- Burning candles takes the edge off a cold room.
- Layer clothes; invest in thermal base layers, or gym leggings and long-sleeved tops are good alternatives.
- Wear a hat and fingerless gloves.
- Use a plug-in heater to get the kids up and at 'em in the morning.
- Hot water bottles are cheap and effective.
- Sit together in one room.
- Use a dehumidifier, damp traps or salt bowls to protect against damp and mould.
- When the sun is out, fully open blinds and curtains to warm your space naturally.
- Take a break every hour to get moving.
- Go somewhere warm if it gets unbearable.
- When all else fails, go to bed early.

CHAPTER 8

LOOK STYLISH FOR LESS

Buying second-hand gives me a thrill. There's a certain clandestine, dopamine boosting, magical feeling in grabbing an item of clothing that's new with a tag or that you know would have cost hundreds of pounds originally and parting only with a few quid for it. Nothing compares to that rush of excitement. An article published in *Good Housekeeping* cited that the average British woman spends £94,000 on clothes in her lifetime. Imagine what you could save if you started thrifting now!

Even before thrifting was a thing, I was buying second-hand – it was needs must as a fashion-savvy teenager.

I feel like thrifting is in my blood. I can't walk past a charity shop or boot sale without having to scratch the itch and get elbow deep in often slightly forlorn-looking and pungent clothes. Thrifting doesn't feel like regular shopping: you don't get that shopping hangover, the bank balance remorse, you don't limit yourself to safe items because of cost, and most of all you get an altogether different thrill. It feels like a hunt, a triumph, to dig your hand deep into a pile of clothes and emerge triumphant with a Joseph dress that would retail for £400 or a £700 Chloé jacket. Who throws this stuff away?

Not everyone gets it. And there's a definite knack to it. I'm hoping that by the time that you have read this I can persuade you to try making *second*-hand your *first* choice, even for a month.

SECOND-HAND VIRTUES

When I started thrifting in the late 1980s, saving the planet wasn't as high on the social and political agenda as it is today. Being environmentally friendly wasn't mainstream – it was for eco warriors with dreadlocks and alternative types who had chosen a bohemian lifestyle. Society has moved on and, armed with science and evidence of a planet that has been ravaged by man's vast appetite for consumables, we are all conscious that we need to do our bit. Whether it's diligently recycling your rubbish or choosing an electric bike or car, aiming to reduce your carbon footprint is the norm now. Unbeknown to me, through my love of second-hand, I had quietly been living the life of a clothes obsessed eco champion.

"Try making *second*-hand your *first* choice."

The Waste & Resources Action Programme (WRAP) estimate that around £30 billion worth of clothing sits unloved in wardrobes up and down the UK (Oh my! I would have a field day!), and £140 million of that goes to landfill or is incinerated. WRAP also claim that extending the life of a single garment by just nine months can reduce its carbon footprint by up to 30%. That's what you do when you buy a piece of preloved clothing – you help in the battle to produce less waste.

I am a living, breathing hangover from the decadent nineties rave scene, and have overcome numerous addictions over the years. Sadly, my love of clothes and shopping is still my Achilles' heel. If I had actually purchased all of the lovely things that I have added to online baskets over the years, I would be bankrupt, my house would have been repossessed and my children would be eating thin gruel.

Today's influencer culture feeds this addiction and creates needs and wants that I didn't know existed until I clicked on the bloody link. I adore Trinny Woodall – her exuberant sense of style, her knowledge and her vast wardrobe hook me into watching her vlogs. She may casually mention her wonderful new Prada sweater and Dries Van Noten coat, and as soon as I google them and see the prices I start to compare myself to her and feel like I have failed at life a bit. There is no way that a working mum on a mid-range salary can shop like a millionaire influencer without serious financial repercussions. This is where thrifting comes into its own.

By buying preloved you can curate a wardrobe of infinite possibilities: you can replicate a look, come up with a totally new look, and most of all experiment and dress to suit how you are feeling. You can do all this at a fraction of the price, and once an item has outlived its welcome in your closet you can give it away, sell it or send it back to the charity shop for someone else to enjoy.

If you are paying £4 for a thrifted garment you are so much more likely to take risks with what you buy and how you style it. If each new piece of clothing that you buy costs at least £30–£50, you tend to err on the side of caution as it's more of an investment. If you wear a second-hand item that cost £4 on four occasions, the cost per wear is just £1; apply this calculation to a £40 item and you can see how buying second-hand stacks up.

SHOP YOUR OWN WARDROBE

While buying second-hand is a sustainable and economical way of creating new looks and styles, even more sustainable is to shop your own wardrobe.

If you are like me and stand in front of your wardrobe with a deep sense of overwhelm, the practice of shopping your own wardrobe takes some major motivation to start and quite a bit of effort to maintain. The basic principles are that you declutter and reorganise your clothes by evaluating what you wear most, which items light up your soul, and which ones remain crumpled and unloved (often with tags) hiding in the bottom of the wardrobe like dirty shopping secrets. The stages, in a nutshell, are:

- **Declutter.** Mercilessly get rid of anything that you won't wear, doesn't fit, doesn't suit, needs repair or was purchased online at 11pm after half a bottle of wine.
- **Take stock.** Audit what you have left. There are apps such as Save Your Wardrobe and Stylebook that enable you to upload pictures of all your clothes so you can play around with outfit ideas. You can also upload pictures of outfits you feel inspired by and it will match your own clothes and aim to replicate.
- **Reinvent.** Play dress-up for big people. Try on colour and pattern combinations that you wouldn't normally consider and create new outfits from the "stock" of your own wardrobe

- **Shop.** The last stage of shopping your own wardrobe is to get your shop on and buy selective items that would tie outfits together and fill in the wardrobe blanks in order to create multiple outfit options.

Thrifting toolkit

Second-hand clothes have nearly always been worn. There is no disputing that, and when someone moves an item along, depending on where you have sourced it, you may be initially put off by the condition. However, I have successfully raised the shabbiest of coats and jumpers from the depth of clothes despair to enjoy a happy few years in my wardrobe. I recommend getting together a thrifting toolkit to get the most out of this most enjoyable of activities. Part of this toolkit will form an emergency rescue for salvaging clothes that on first inspection look ready for retirement; part of it will be for styling your thrifted finds, as on occasion it does require some imagination and restyling to make things work.

Your **thrifting toolkit** should ideally contain the following items:

- **Journal or notebook** – To take a mini audit of your wardrobe and the items that you REALLY need to source to create multiple looks.
- **Rechargeable electronic debobbling gadget** – This will become your best friend. You can take a jumper that looks fit for the dog's bed and after 10 minutes of shaving with the magic debobbler it's good to go again for a few years. I have one from Amazon that cost £10.

- **Small sharp scissors** – For removing dangly loose threads.
- **Small sewing kit** – I am completely devoid of sewing talent, but a small kit is useful for tightening buttons, or putting the odd stitch in a hem or under an arm.
- **Stain removal products** – Elbow Grease Bar, Vanish, Spray bleach or Bicarbonate of Soda.
- **Deodorisers** – My go-to favourite is Fabulosa Spray & Wear. Some preloved items, even when washed, can retain l'aroma de charity shop. A quick spritz freshens them up and gets rid of any lingering mustiness.
- **Potent fabric softeners** – For making preloved clothes smell like yours after the first wash.
- **Antibacterial spray** – You can't really wash shoes, bags and jewellery, so for hygiene reasons I would recommend spraying them thoroughly with an antibac spray. Again I love the Fabulosa range as they smell really good so get rid of both musty smells and germs.
- **Inner soles** – Preferably in thin leather or they don't impact the fit, these will protect your delicate trotters from coming into direct contact of the inside sole of used footwear.
- **Large reusable bag** – To carry your treasure home as charity shops often don't have bags available.
- **Wide stretchy belt** – You will need at least one of these, and you may need to invest in a new one initially (black is safest). I have been lucky enough to curate a collection of preloved belts over the years. With the magic of a stretchy belt you can shop outside your size, widening the opportunity to rescue preowned dresses.

SOURCING PRELOVED TREASURE

I love clothes, I love the thrill of a bargain and the opportunity to try new colours, patterns and silhouettes. I have never had a large disposable income, and find that shopping in regular stores – whether it be on the high street or online – doesn't give me the variety that I would like in my wardrobe. Shelling out for brand-new goods means that most mere mortals have to stick to a budget, and this means that you don't take risks with your money. The same safe bets, core pieces and basic colours are repurchased time and time again, and you get stuck in a wardrobe rut. You see images online or in magazines of whole outfits accessorised with belts, shoes, necklaces and other items to give a "pop of colour"; then you look at the prices listed in the editorial and, with a sigh, resign yourself with, "I could just get the black trousers." You feel stuck in a groove with no scope to experiment. This is where thrifting opens up a world of dressing opportunity.

"If I could bottle the feeling you get when you bag a fabulous second-hand bargain I would be a millionaire."

You never quite know what you will find and for how much – but if I could bottle the feeling you get when you bag a fabulous second-hand bargain I would be a millionaire.

Prices vary depending on where you source your preloved goodies. In today's internet age, there are infinite options for sourcing preloved clothes, from online auctions and resale websites, national and local Facebook selling groups, Instagram, charity shops, boots sales and swap parties. In this chapter, I will run through the different ways to source great second-hand clothes, and share the pitfalls, tricks and tips I have gleaned over my many years of buying preloved clothes. Here's to happy shopping everywhere!

SWAP AND SHOP
Swap parties

The first port of call for saving money and being eco conscious is to swap and shop your own wardrobe, and there are a few ways you can start doing this. One of the simplest and most fun is to lure a group of like-minded friends with gin and nibbles, and request that they all bring a few items from their wardrobe that they are just not in love with any more. I suggest that you set a value range, as it's a bit skewed if the people you invite all shop at Harvey Nichols and you shop at Primark. So to avoid any conflict or embarrassment, maybe set a value range for clothing, another for shoes, and another for accessories. You and your pals simply lay out the items that you have all bought and you can either offer up swaps for items, or just pick up what takes your fancy. If more than one of you likes the same thing, then you could maybe suggest sharing the item if you live locally to each other or... handbags at dawn! You can theme the parties – for example, jewellery or dresses, or shoes and handbags – as this can make it easier for you all to do the initial wardrobe cull at home.

Online swaps

There are a number of formal and informal ways to swap clothes online. This will involve posting unless you are located in the same town or city. I have listed a few of the current apps that are available for swapping below, and I am sure that as the "slow fashion" movement gains momentum more will pop up.

- **Nuw (nuwardrobe.com & app)** – Users upload photos of clothes that they wish to swap or lend to the app and earn "coins" every time they list an item. The coins act as credits toward getting a swap from the app (each item costs 99p).
- **Vinted (vinted.co.uk & app)** – A well-established selling site that also allows users to opt to swap or sell items. The user profile notifies you as to whether they will accept swaps as well as straight purchases.
- **Dopplle (dopplle.com & app)** – This has a narrower audience as it's aimed at students. Again, users simply upload their items and browse for items that they would like to swap.
- **Facebook groups (facebook.com & app)** – These are a bit more organic in nature than downloadable apps. One of my most trusted and favourite is Clobber Swap (clobberswap. co.uk) which is a very active women's only group.

CAR BOOT SALES

For me, car boot sales are the holy grail of second-hand clothes shopping. Of course, you can get everything and anything at a car boot sale – not just clothes. You never know from week to week what you will find; you may have boom weeks when you take home a bag overflowing with wondrous finds, or lean weeks when you come home with nothing.

The typical car boot season is March to September. In the height of summer, there can be hundreds of cars lined up, boots aloft and trestle tables erected, ready to sell on unwanted goodies. In winter, pickings are slimmer – dark mornings and inclement weather are enough to put off the fair weather booters and both seller and buyer numbers dwindle.

Before you go

- **Check details.** Make sure you know the location and start and finish times. Facebook is probably a better place to check than an actual Google search, as less-established boot sales may not have any web presence.
- **Plan your itinerary.** Once you have checked times, it's worth planning ahead to see if you can visit several boot sales on one day. Opening times may be staggered, enabling you to cram in even more thrifting.
- **Weather.** If you wake up to torrential rain then outdoor boot sales are more often than not cancelled. But don't be put off by light rain or drizzle – there may be less sellers than there would be on a blistering summer morning, but those that persevere will be keen to get rid of everything. No one wants to reload the car with damp clothes, books and bric-a-brac. These sellers will be on a mission to get rid of everything, which means that they may be willing to let go of items for rock-bottom prices. And, yes, I really am talking prices as low as 10p.
- **Cash.** Decide on your budget spend for the day. Draw your cash out and find a local shop happy to give you lots of £1 coins in your change… You need £1 and 50p coins ideally, as early on sellers won't have enough change to take your notes. As the day progresses, they will amass lots of change

in their bum bags, but early on you may miss out on a bargain if they can't give you change from a note.

- **Bags.** You want to have your hands free to be able to rummage in piles of clothing with wild abandon. Keep your cash, phone, keys (anything you don't want to lose) in a cross-body bag and keep it zipped up.
  - o The best bags to carry your boot sale treasure in are those large zippable laundry type bags. As sellers at boot sales use open bags to keep items for sale in by their stall, an open bag full of bought treasure is easily mistaken for items for sale by other buyers. To avoid embarrassing conflicts with other buyers, keep your bag zipped and close to you.

When you arrive

I recommend getting to a boot sale just as it opens, but no need to get there early to head up the queue – what will be will be, treasure that's meant for you will be found. There are, of course, stalwart resellers (those who make their money finding bargains and selling them on at a profit) that queue up an hour in advance. Often a klaxon or horn is sounded, and they sprint toward the tables and stalls. I kid you not! This behaviour is not becoming for a thrifting duchess – hell, this is meant to be dignified fun!

Traders

Often selling from large vans or lorries, traders sell anything from fidget spinners to out-of-date pet food. They are often located together in one area of the boot sale. I tend to walk straight past these stalls and head for the sellers who appear to be regular householders having a Marie Kondo moment – this is where the best clothing bargains are.

Look for clues

There isn't any need to invest huge amounts of time rigorously checking every single item of clothing on every single seller's pitch – there are often killer clues that give away that there are potential bargains to be had. These are not failsafe, but reliable the majority of the time.

- **Bags.** Look at the bags the seller has used to transport their wares. If you spy Harvey Nichols, John Lewis, House of Fraser, Flannels, Zara or Waitrose bags it gives you an indication that they have higher-end goodies for sale.
- **Cars.** This is a bit hit and miss as young girls will drive a clapped-out jalopy and spend their wages on nights out and clothes, which they tire of quickly. Equally, that top of the range Mercedes SUV could be leased and the driver neck deep in credit agreements with no disposable income. A fancy new car doesn't always indicate that the seller will have great clothes for sale.
- **Sellers.** I am unsure whether I have a canny sixth sense or buyer's intuition, but sometimes you just know. I scan bags and faces and outfits. Even though boot sales start early, you can often tell by someone's coat, footwear and hair whether they are a good match for you. I am not suggesting you walk around psychologically profiling sellers by their appearance, but if you're going to stop at a seller's pitch and spend time

having a really good delve, it's worth considering, "Would I wear their coat? Would I wear those shoes?" etc. In short, do you like their image?

Get over the "ick"

What puts most car boot rookies off a good mooch is the thought of clothes being worn by someone else, whether this be for hygiene reasons, or snobbery about buying second-hand. Admittedly, there will be some pitches at the car boot sale where you can smell damp garage or attic on the approach, but the majority of sellers literally lift their unwanted clothes from their wardrobe and drawers and pile them into a black bin bag or suitcase. They are 95% of the time laundered, sometimes you strike gold and they will be ironed too. The ick factor, the fear that somehow it's dirty, is just perception. If the clothes smell musty or fusty, just walk away and move to the next pitch. The majority are washday fresh. I mean who literally wants to air their dirty laundry in public?

Top & bottom test

Car boot sales can be big summer events, with a huge number of pitches. To limit the time I spend at pitches where I am going to come away empty-handed, I do the top and bottom test: check the top and bottom of the pile to suss whether they have good quality items or cheap supermarket clothes and make a quick assessment whether it's worth 10 minutes of my rummaging time.

Haggle without ego

The best bit about car boot sales is the haggling. If someone asks for £3, offer a £1, usually you will meet in the middle, but you need to drop any ego. There is a temptation to cut your nose off to spite your face and walk away if they stick to their guns, but if you are haggling over a £200 coat for £3 and you know it's a steal, go with it, drop your pride and concede. This is no time for being stubborn or prideful – the coat will not be there when you go back round. You don't have to "win" when you are haggling, and your ego could stop you bagging a once in a lifetime bargain.

CHARITY SHOPS

Charity shops have not escaped the grip of the cost of living crisis; hence they are number two on my list of great places to source thrifted clothes. Seasoned thrifters, myself included, are collectively bemoaning the insanely steep cost of items in charity shops; with the rising cost of energy, transporting items, rents and wages, they have no choice but to pass the additional costs on to shoppers.

I am not writing charity shops off altogether, but you have to be prepared to have a good rummage. A Primark top tagged at £7.99 in a charity shop is not a bargain, but a Whistles dress that originally cost £140 is. You need to shop savvy and be prepared to hunt, as there are nearly always good deals nestled among the fast-fashion tat.

Even when I come back from a charity shop empty-handed, which isn't often as there is always a book for 50p or a bone-handled butter knife that I need for my collection, it is an hour or two well spent. There is something mindful about thrifting in charity shops – you lose yourself in the rails, forget anything that was troubling you, and become immersed in the search. Even if the charity shop gods are not on your side, it is time out of a usually frenetic routine, just for you.

Expect the unexpected

Curating a wardrobe from charity shop finds takes a little more time and patience as you never know what you will find when you are thrifting. If you have a special event and need something fancy, there are no guarantees that you will find that perfect item when you go out thrifting as stock is so random. Charity shops do, however, rotate their stock seasonally, so if you have a black tie event in the middle of summer ask whether they are holding any evening wear. The shop may have limited floor space and be only displaying high summer gear; they may just have the perfect item waiting in the wings. If you see a killer item at a bargain charity shop price and you know that it is something you will use in future or works with your wardrobe, I recommend snapping it up as you most probably will not see it again. I have so many regrets when I have walked away from chazza shop finds because I was dithering over a few quid and returned to see someone else holding my coveted item in their clammy mitts.

"There is something mindful about thrifting in charity shops."

I would also recommend mooching through all the sections, as often stock gets muddled by shoppers in store and staff can accidently misgender items too. Men's jackets can work well as ladies' blazers, and some teenage clothing fits a size smaller adults perfectly well.

Fashion trends change so quickly – hell! We even have micro trends now – and the alarming rate at which people discard and donate clothes means that there is genuinely something for everyone in charity shops. You do need to use a bit of imagination, sometimes improvise, and most definitely be willing to see beyond some of the tatty, budget supermarket brands on offer but there is definitely treasure on those rails.

I often browse some of my favourite stores' websites for inspiration and to see what they have on offer for the current season. I am now convinced, in my advancing years, that there are only so many conceivable permutations of trousers, skirts, jackets, tops and shoes. Is anything in fashion today truly original or new? Charity shops offer such a vast array and variety of clothes that you most certainly will find something very similar to what is being sold as new stock by big retailers.

Pricing & layout

Charity shops all have their own way of merchandising and pricing their wares. Some arrange stock into clothing type: a rail for skirts, a rail for jeans, one for tops, one for dresses; others arrange clothing in sizes, and others by colour. I find the easiest to navigate are those that arrange by clothing type, as I never rule out shopping outside my size. A good waist-cinching belt can bring a dress down several sizes (especially oversized flounce-type frocks) – so go for it if you like the print or shape.

Pricing can also vary vastly from shop to shop. City-centre shops, with higher business rates and rents will, of course, pass that cost on to shoppers, so I much prefer to shop at out-of-town, local-to-area charity shops. They don't have the same wage overheads or infrastructure as national charities: CEOs, regional managers, marketing executives, and social media and campaign managers.

They usually represent smaller local charities where the majority of the profit goes straight to helping local people or animals. My personal favourite is an animal sanctuary charity shop in a village 5 miles from home; it operates for a small charity, with just one animal shelter, so I know that most of the money I spend goes toward helping rehome cats and dogs (I am a sucker for a sad furry face).

Large charities are super-savvy when it comes to pricing: they research brands and ticket them accordingly. Their job is to raise as much revenue that they can for the charity and, armed with Google, they can quickly gauge what something is worth. Occasionally, a lesser-known but expensive brand can slip through the net, and I always feel giddy with excitement when I find a covetable treasure that the staff have clearly mispriced. Often, national charities will cream off the very best and sell it online to reach a wider audience. Some, like Oxfam, have their own websites; others have well established eBay stores.

The more local shops offer much richer pickings for designer bargains, especially shops in leafy, affluent suburbs. I veer toward these as the odds of finding high-quality clothes for a fraction of their original retail price are much higher.

Research

Don't be embarrassed to get your phone out mid-mooch to check the value or provenance of a piece. I do this all the time. If an item has a hand stitched label, a silk lining or just feels like exceptional quality, I will google the label or take a snap of it in Google Lens to gauge whether I have struck gold. My best find was a Maria Grachvogel dress for £3.75. It was silk lined and the label oozed quality but I hadn't heard of it. I quickly researched the label in the shop and saw that her dresses retail for around £2,500 new! It is one of my most valuable finds yet.

Great buys

There are some charity shop buys that are great wardrobe basics; these have very little hanger appeal and are easily overlooked. Faced with a cacophony of mixed colours and prints when thrifting, it is easy to skim past good quality, essential black dresses, trousers and tops, and white and cream blouses and jeans. They can get lost in the swathes of bright and bold clothes on the rails, and it is always worth taking time to rummage through to unearth high-end wardrobe basics. I have found pricey J Brand jeans, Joseph silk blouses and vintage Helmut Lang by taking extra time to peruse the, on first glance, dull basic items on the rails.

I have a finely tuned radar that can spot a bit of cashmere or silk a mile off. Good quality knits and fabrics nestled among the rails of cheaper high-street fashion are thrifters' gold. Always look for great textures and prints.

> **"Good quality knits and fabrics nestled among the rails of cheaper high-street fashion are thrifters' gold."**

I always start by standing back from the rail and dive in to the spot that catches my eye first. I prefer long dresses, and standing back allows me to identify lengths very quickly without having to dissect the whole rail. I then do the label flick. I quickly thumb through the rails at hanger level looking for designer labels. I will, of course, buy a Sainsbury's jumper if I love everything about it, but I am all about getting the most bang for my buck.

I recommend hunting down great belts, bags and accessories. If you can't afford a full outfit, then accessories can amp up what you already own, and a selection of different coloured bags and belts can make all the difference to a plain outfit. Buying these finishing touches brand new can quickly tot up the cost of an outfit, but buying them preloved raises your game for a fraction of the cost.

Haggle & repair

If you find a killer item in a charity shop missing a button, with a loose hem, a stain, mark or a pull, don't be put off. I am always cheeky and point the flaw out to staff and ask whether I can buy it for a discount. Staff usually quality control when they put stock out, but it may be one that they have missed and would otherwise have put in the rag bag. I would say that 99% of the time I can remove stains with a mixture of Vanish and bicarbonate of soda or bleach; I can shave off pulls with my debobbler; and small repairs are doable, even for an unskilled seamstress like me. Take a punt, they usually pay off.

ONLINE

There used to only be eBay for second-hand clothes online; now there is a plethora of resale sites and even big online retailers like ASOS, Zara and H&M are targeting the resale market to tick their sustainability box. The most popular online platforms are: eBay, Vinted, Depop and Vestiaire, with Poshmark also launching in the UK in 2023. My current favourite is Vinted, as I just don't have the patience to get caught up in an auction on eBay. Vinted allows you to make the seller offers, and is so easy to use. To bag the best bargains, I always search "newest" first in the item that I am looking for. The bargains get snapped up very quickly so by searching the new listings you can weed out the rock-bottom prices. Searching "newest" first is the virtual equivalent to being on the sale shop floor when they wheel out a rail of bargains. Searching by price from low to high gives you lots of lower price-listings to peruse, but not necessarily the great-quality listings.

The resale market is booming with people buying preloved for sustainable as well as economic reasons. New ventures focused on serving up second-hand loveliness are launching all the time. Some of my favourites are Thrift+ and b.kinda. Some specialise in vintage clothing, others for the plus-size market. There really is something for everyone, and online shops are a great solution for anyone unable to leave home to visit a car boot sale or charity shop in person.

Flipping your wardrobe

One of the best things about online resale sites is that you can, if you are canny, dress for free. That's right – for free! If I tire of my thrifted finds, I try and resell them online for the same as, if not more, than I originally paid for them. This way, my wardrobe is kept up to date, clothes remain in use and circulation, and I can shop guilt-free from the proceeds of my sales. If items do not sell, I will flog the remainder for very low prices at a car boot, and anything that is left then gets donated to charity shops. It's a win-win: someone gets something new to them and you get money to buy something else.

TOP TAKEAWAYS
LOOK STYLISH FOR LESS

- Swap clothes with friends to update your wardrobe.
- Prepare yourself for thrifting by assembling a Thrifting Toolkit.
- Visit car boot sales for the cheapest thrifted finds.
- Visit out-of-town, local charity shops for the biggest bargains.
- Look for quality fabrics and labels.
- Use Google Lens to reverse search the provenance of items.
- Sell unworn clothes to fund future shopping trips.

CHAPTER 9

THRIFTY GIFTS, SPECIAL OCCASIONS & CELEBRATIONS

Whatever celebrations busy up your annual calendar, you can bet your bottom dollar (quite literally) that it will cost you a lot of money. Whether it be Diwali, Easter, Eid, Hanukkah, Christmas or Guru Nanak Day, it's going to involve cost. Exchanging gifts, decorating our homes and preparing a feast doesn't come cheap. The one thing that you can be certain of with these big celebrations is that they happen every year, so with some planning and nifty-thrifty thinking you can celebrate with loved ones on a budget.

There is a pressure, usually driven by social media and our favourite influencers and celebrities, to have photo-op worthy themed decorations and sumptuous overindulgent feasts, to wear coordinated outfits and give extravagant gifts. Lives are curated into little Instagram grids, and new impossible standards of perfect are being set. This, of course, usually has nothing to do with the true meaning of the celebration; surely the meaning of *any* gathering to celebrate with friends and family is love and connection. In a difficult economic climate, when so many of us are stretched financially, it seems tone deaf to set the gift bar impossibly high. It certainly isn't a celebration if you have maxed out your overdraft or credit cards to create the illusion of bottomless wealth. Remember, a lot of the products those bloggers, celebs and influencers are showcasing have probably been gifted by the companies with the aim of selling them to you.

GIFTS

As a full-time working mum, I was driven by guilt to overindulge my little darlings with gifts when they were small to ease my conscience about working. I can remember my son's first Christmas. He was nine months old and I wanted to make it special. He already had everything that a nine-month-old could possibly need in his life, and I actually struggled to know what to buy him to make sure that he had a huge pile of gifts under the tree. Family also asked me what they could buy for him, and I had no clue what to ask for. I wandered aimlessly around Toys R Us and filled a trolley with soft toys, talking toys, Dora the Explorer dolls, Igglepiggles and various other overpriced toys. I totted up a grand total of £400, and wrapped them up feeling satisfied that he had a gargantuan mountain of gifts to plough through. Christmas Day came and it took him hours to open them. He would open a toy and want to play with it, but we were moving him gently on to the next gift (that Christmas dinner wasn't going to cook itself). He was totally overwhelmed, and his favourite gifts ended up being a £5 pull-back car and a cuddly toy. The other toys didn't get much of a look in, and I realised at that moment that all of the extra money that I had spent would probably have been better off invested in a trust fund for when he really needed it. The moral of this story is: I bought stuff for the sake of it, to keep up with the Joneses, to post that obligatory "Father Christmas has been" photograph on Facebook displaying an obscene 5-foot mountain of gifts.

"Any gift-giving agreement or pledge needs to be agreed between friends and family."

There is something soul destroying about rushing around town with a tick list of names, buying gifts because you have to "get the job done". It feels like a chore – there is no real thought or love invested, and you may be limited to whatever is in stock or available at the time. It will always feel way more personal to give a gift that you have spotted at leisure, that you know will mean something special to the recipient – this is how to derive joy from gifting and shopping for gifts. In my bid to take the horrendous pressure off our biggest celebration, Christmas, I have organically developed a set of strategies to enjoy a thrifty Christmas, which can of course apply whatever the occasion.

GIFT PLEDGES

Any gift-giving agreement or pledge needs to be agreed between friends and family. There is nothing worse than turning up empty-handed on the presumption there was a no gift policy, only to be gifted a beauty gift box or a helicopter experience. Pledges work on a sliding scale, depending on your collective level of skintness or your shared level of aversion to marketing-driven overconsumption.

Kids only

As adults we don't really *need* stuff; we have clothes on our backs, food in our bellies and a roof over our heads. We often struggle to think of things for people to buy us – how many times has a friend or relative asked you what you would like for Christmas and you have no clue. Multiply this by several requests and you are clutching at straws, desperately adding things to a Christmas list that you neither need, nor really want. The magic of receiving gifts wanes as we get older, especially when you have had to rack your brains to even think of some abstract item that you might need. Take the pressure off all sides by agreeing to only buy gifts for children. You will need to agree together what constitutes a child, but your cousin Steve who is 40 and lives at home definitely doesn't qualify. Agreeing to buy gifts only for children dramatically reduces your Christmas budget *and* takes out about 70% of the pre-Christmas stress.

Agree a budget

If you are wedded to buying gifts for adults as well as children, agree a specific budget. Whether it be £5, £10 or £20, having a tighter budget inspires you to get creative with your gift giving. If you are creative, paint something, knit some socks or arm warmers, or gift a plant in an upcycled pot; put your crafty skills to use and give a gift made with love.

Once you have agreed the gift budget, stick to it. Although we don't give to receive, there is something mortifying when there is a huge disparity in the value of gifts being exchanged.

Gift your time

A thrifty alternative to giving gifts with a financial cost is a time swap. Gifting your time or skills is a great way to help someone out and to get help tackling irksome tasks that you have been putting off yourself. We all have unique skills and talents that could benefit someone else, and you can either agree a nominal value in hours or a favour for a favour. For example:

- decluttering or cleaning
- fixing a leaky tap
- revamping a CV
- gardening
- small car repairs
- decorating a room
- clearing out an attic
- cooking a nice meal
- knitting, sewing or baking

The list is endless, and you will need to think about what you can offer and where you could benefit from a helping hand. It really can be as simple as spring cleaning or baking a cake.

PRELOVED PERFECTION

Who says that gifts need to be brand-spanking-new shiny things from online or high-street stores? It will come as no surprise that I am a huge fan of thrifting. Charity shops, car boot sales, Vinted, eBay, to name a few sources are full of absolute gems – and not just clothing – many of which *are* brand new.

On the whole, people consume more of everything than we did 20 years ago. The demise of bricks-and-mortar shops and 24/7 access to almost anything online means that people are shopping more and more from the comfort of their own home. The good old-fashioned changing room has been replaced by the try on at home and return. This is great news for fans of shopping preowned as a huge proportion of people miss return dates or are simply too lazy to return unwanted purchases.

The sheer volume of stuff that I pick up second-hand that is BNWT or BNIB (brand new with tags or brand new in box – I actually use these as search terms online) is insane. For a fraction of the retail price, I have found current-season Zara sweaters, branded costume jewellery, handbags, shoes, scarves and toiletries all brand new and sealed – perfect to give as gifts.

Alternatively, you don't need to find a tagged item to gift. I collect unused items from beauty gift boxes in charity shops and at boot sales and make up pamper boxes (check to ensure products are in date, of course). Books are seldom read more than once, so there are lots in almost new condition in charity shops. Gently used quality clothes and accessories in luxury fabrics like cashmere, silk and leather also make fabulous gifts, as do good quality vintage clothing finds.

Last year 50% of the gifts that I gave were preloved. The recipient was not even initially aware that they had been sourced second-hand. I did reveal this later and everyone was unanimously impressed by the quality of the goodies that I had found. These included a necklace with a £60 price tag for £2, a cashmere scarf (listed on Vestiaire for £160) for £1.99 and clothes from various high-street stores. My daughter received a huge pamper kit that was made up of car-booted GLOSSYBOX and Birchbox (subscription-based beauty companies) bits that I had found at car boot sales. Buying second-hand helped stretch my gift budget so much further than if I had purchased all new gifts. The added bonus is that you are supporting a charity or helping someone else to make a few quid, and being sustainable at the same time.

And you can even suggest a gift pledge to *all* buy preloved gifts, again with or without a fixed budget.

SHOP ALL YEAR

To purchase only budget-friendly or thrifted gifts, you can't wait until the last minute. Shopping all year round to build up a heathy collection of affordable gifts is the answer. Every time you're at a car boot sale or in a charity shop, keep your eyes peeled for giftable items that you can add to your pressie drawer. If you see something and think, "Ooh my sister would love that," but her birthday isn't for another four months, just grab it anyway and store it until the special occasion.

"Shop all year round to build up a collection of gifts."

It may feel a bit ambitious to start shopping for gifts in January, particularly when you've just got Christmas done and dusted, but January sales are the *best* for picking up bargains for impromptu gifts to use throughout the year. Boots 75% off sale anyone? This usually happens in the third week of January, and you can tell when it's going to happen as the prices online switch over at midnight the night before. I pick up kid-friendly gifts, so when the kids are invited to birthday parties I can avoid having to rush out and buy an emergency last-minute present. Lip gloss sets, bathing sets, mugs and socks, make-up brushes – and even the foodie gifts – are all great year-round presents.

Even when it's still freezing outside, retailers will be clearing Christmas and winter stock to make way for spring season goodies. This is your time to pounce, especially for Christmas gifts. Nightwear, scarves, gloves and thick socks are never not going to be useful.

I like to keep a list of names ready – family, friends, the kids' best friends – and mark out birthdays and other occasions when you are likely to give a gift. You could even include end-of-term favourite teacher gifts. This way you can shop at leisure, searching out the best second-hand or sale bargains, and avoid that awful last-minute panic buying.

FREEBIES & GIVEAWAYS

I love making up pamper gift boxes – probably because I would be delighted to receive one myself! I have mastered the art of bagging freebies to create beauty boxes worth hundreds of pounds, just for the price of the postage. I scour social media – Facebook and Instagram are particularly great for this – to find posts where companies are offering free, full-sized samples for the cost of postage. My most recent finds have been a £60 moisturiser for £4.99, a £50 serum for £3.25, a £40 eye cream for £4.25 and a free body care set. Packaged up together in nice wrapping, the combined price of all of these goodies made a fabulous luxury gift worth £150 for £12.50.

To do this successfully you need to collect freebies all year round. Make sure that you have a recipient in mind, so you are not just getting caught up in a freebie frenzy (I must admit, I do get my own skincare in this way too, so nothing is ever wasted). It does mean wasting a bit of time on social media, but I am guilty of this anyway – I may as well be doing something useful while watching funny cat videos. The companies I have found offers from recently are Skin Chemists, Flânerie, Dr Botanicals, Avant, Murad and Dead Sea Dream. Simply follow skincare companies for offers to pop up.

I also enter a ton of Instagram competitions, and keep any prizes I win to give as gifts. Last year, I won jewellery, clothing, skincare and accessories worth hundreds of pounds. Usually you have to like a post and tag friends. I suggest agreeing with some friends that they will be your competition buddies so they don't get fed up with you tagging them in every competition going.

Even if you are not a fan of Instagram, it is worth setting up an account for the giveaways. Lots of micro-influencers are gifted products to promote and often they are gifted additional products to give away so that the brand gets followers. You can follow and unfollow people and companies at your leisure, so there really isn't anything to lose.

If you look at the amount of likes on a giveaway post, it gives you a clue to your odds of winning. Often there will be less than a thousand likes, which is pretty good odds in my book.

Search for #giveawaysUK, #giveway, #competitions, #freebies, to find recent posts with goodies to claim. I had literally never won anything in my life until I started entering Instagram giveaways. But with so many available and with such good odds, I have had a pretty good yield in the last 12 months. I set an hour aside one evening a week and enter all the giveaways and competitions that I can find.

GIFT WRAP

PRELOVED & RE-LOVED

I am a bit evangelistic when it comes to packaging, but for good reason. It just makes so much sense to repurpose pre-used gift boxes, bags and baskets. It's not as if they are used for long. A gift is placed inside and it is opened, usually carefully (unless my gremlin children get their hands on it; they even tear the sides off cereal boxes!), leaving it pristine. Last year, I purchased all of my gift boxes to make up pamper kits from a local charity shop. They were 50p each, the retail price of a large fancy box is much pricier.

You can also get creative with wicker baskets and fabric scraps. I recently attended a sustainability fayre and a lovely lady approached me and gave me some pretty scraps of fabric. It was tradition in her home to wrap small gifts in squares of fabric tied up with a bow. I tried it with the fabric she gave me and it looked rather rustic and pretty – and, best of all, could be reused. Hessian, muslin squares, old bedding and clothes can be cut up with pinking shears (those scissors that create a zigzag edge) to make gorgeous gift wrapping. It's thrifty and sustainable and looks pretty too.

SUPER SALES

If you do need to buy gift wrap, the January sales are your go-to. Stock up on the most non-Christmassy wrap that you can find. I found white wrap with a tropical jungle print in which the animals were wearing very discreet festive hats – you would have needed to really analyse the paper with a magnifying class to identify it as being Christmas-themed. Buying a non-Christmassy Christmas paper means that you can get away with using it all year round. I stocked up on enough rolls at 40p each to last me through a year of gift giving.

DELEGATE TO THE KIDS

A great way to get the kids involved and give gifts in really personalised wrapping is to make your own. If you have old rolls of lining paper (for walls) to hand, get the kids on board with gift giving by getting them to decorate it. It's a great way of keeping the kids occupied on a rainy afternoon.

DECORATIONS

USE WHAT YOU HAVE

Repeat after me: "I do not need to buy new, colour coordinated decorations every year. I am not a celebrity, I do not have the income that most celebs do, and it's wasteful to replace perfectly good decorations with new ones."

Make sure that lights, baubles, banners, trees and hangings are carefully packaged away. Lights can be wound round a pringles tube or a cardboard box and should be kept somewhere dry and accessible where they won't get damp or bashed. Reusing what you have already is the thriftiest way to decorate your home.

SWAP SHOP

If you are bored of your decs and fancy the novelty of "new to you", why not host a decoration swap with friends. It's a good excuse to get together over a glass of something warming and have fun swapping decorations to re-theme your home for a big celebration. You can always swap back afterwards if some of your decs have sentimental value.

Birthday banners are a massive waste of money and usually made of foiled plastic that's terrible for the environment. As they are generally used for one day only, keep an eye out on Freecycle or Facebook "Don't Dump It" groups, as there are usually loads on offer. I've also seen full balloon arches being given away for free. I highly recommend joining all of your local free groups.

GET CRAFTY

Get your Blue Peter on and get crafty by making decorations. This is another fab way of getting the kids involved in preparations while saving money; use junk shop finds or things that you find on outdoor treks and stuff lying around at home. There is lots of inspiration on Pinterest. My kids loved making dough decorations and painting them, and they took great joy in collecting pine cones and twigs when we were out on muddy woodland walks – a can of spray paint and some glue and you're good to go. Once you let the kids loose, anything goes; it's likely you will have to grimace through mismatched and non-symmetrical decorations in all shades of the rainbow. To avoid looking like a day nursery, I would suggest picking a theme and sticking to it, whether it be Nordic and natural, gold and glitzy or traditional. Some of our most treasured decorations are handmade; lovingly dusted off year after year, they never fail to evoke cherished memories.

LIGHT IT UP

If you are not particularly handy with scissors and sticky back tape, never underestimate the power of a fairy light or those newer wire LED lights. Stuffed in jars, draped round houseplants, flanking staircases and surrounding picture frames they instantly create a cosy, festive vibe – and don't look out of place if you can't be arsed to take them down afterwards.

MAKING MERRY

Hosting a party, gathering or meal can cost you an arm and a leg. You could, of course, hibernate until all of the festivities and celebrations are over. I am not by any stretch a massive social butterfly, and could quite happily hunker down with a good book until everything is back to normal, but apparently that's not really socially acceptable. Love it or hate it, at some point you will get roped into making merry. Never one to miss an opportunity to be frugal, I have honed a few hacks to revel on a shoestring.

SHARE THE LOAD

To avoid any cost to yourself whatsoever, you could of course invite yourself to join in with other people's festivities. We all have kith and kin that love organising and hosting others and would welcome an extra seat round the table. Do, of course, offer to bring a bottle of something fizzy or prepare a dessert to take along.

If you are not able to travel to see family on key holidays and celebrations, share the load with friends and neighbours. There seems little point in preparing large meals tucked away in your own homes, using energy, potentially cooking too much and wasting food. Instead, chip in together and join forces. Agree who will host the meal, then split the dishes across guests. That way, you share the cooking, the cost and the camaraderie with close friends. I always do this at Christmas and Easter with my closest friend; she is a single mum, as am I now. It makes sense to bring our families together to share the load. My neighbours are from Mauritius and Ireland and, with no family in town, I extend an invite to them too. The more the merrier – and there is less cooking and cost for you.

BYOB (Bring your own booze)

The most expensive part of hosting a party is buying enough booze to go round and last the night. The simplest way to save a huge chunk off your party budget is to ask guests to bring their own bottle to add to the bar.

BYOD (Bring your own dish)

Most people have one thing that they cook well – their signature dish, their speciality. Mine is my made-up recipe of Korean dirty rice; it always goes down a bomb, is cheap to make and goes a long way. One of my closest friends always whips up her fabulous mackerel pâté, and another brings homemade hummus. Asking all of your guests to bring their signature dish will reduce your shopping budget drastically, and save you time and energy in the kitchen. The added bonus is that you can share recipes and tips and add a few extra dishes to your own culinary repertoire.

Host a "Club Card" party

A "Club Card" party takes some planning, but means that the party can often be totally free. Agree with your guests that you will all use a set amount from your supermarket reward points to pay for party food and drink. You will need to prepare a shopping list and divvy it up among prospective guests ahead of the big day. Everyone brings over their contribution and you all party for free.

HEIDI'S HINTS
VIPS ONLY

The cost of hosting a party can quickly spiral out of control. Nibbles and drinks targeted for a seasonal market are costly and, depending on the number of guests, the cost for party food alone can quickly rack up. Keeping to a modest guest list will help to keep costs down. And remember, text or WhatsApp invites are paper-free and cost-free.

PARTY FUND

If you know in advance that you are planning a party and are on a limited budget, I recommend setting up a saving pot for it. Worrying about the cost of entertaining will suck all of the joy out of the event for you and you probably won't feel as relaxed on the night. There is nothing more stressful than inviting people over in advance and splurging all of your disposable income from one monthly pay check. As soon as your hangover has lifted, you will be staring down the barrel of a very skint month. Instead, decide on your overall budget for the party and save up for it. Don't exceed your budget trying to impress with the best wines, cheese and charcuterie, instead focus on creating great atmosphere with music, lighting and laughter.

THEME

A themed party shifts some of the focus off the food and drink and onto the music, outfits and décor. Choose a decade, sixties, seventies, eighties, gosh even the nineties are vintage now (that makes me feel incredibly old). A hip hop party, a grunge party, a movie-themed party – the world is your oyster. You could pick a country, a continent, a city – in fact, any theme where you can coordinate music, dress and décor. Use Spotify or Amazon Prime Music for tunes, and state that any costumes need to be thrifted to keep the costs down for everyone and to get the imagination flowing. You can also shop second-hand for décor – anything goes when it's an improvised theme party.

By creating a themed cocktail for the party, you can limit the drinks that you need to just that cocktail's ingredients. Themed food also means that you can reduce your nibbles menu. For an Italy-themed party, for example, you could do bruschetta, pizza and a huge vat of Bolognese served with Bellinis, which isn't an expensive menu. You can find plentiful outfit inspiration on Pinterest, from Super Mario to gondoliers, the Pope and Sophia Loren. Let your imagination run wild, and remember it doesn't have to be perfect – improvisation on a budget is the name of the game.

Themes work well for kids' parties. You can take it one step further in warmer weather and take the party outside. There is nothing more stress-inducing than a tribe of pre-teens smearing cake icing into your rugs and soft furnishings, so taking the party outside eliminates all the party carnage and saves money on hiring a venue. As long as you have someone to help you supervise a gaggle of excitable kids, transport the party to your local park, a beach or the woods. Treasure hunts with clues keep the little one's occupied. With a few cut-out pictures strategically hidden, you can create a Gruffalo hunt; or create a pirate treasure hunt adventure on a beach. Just make sure it's rewarding and the treasure isn't too well hidden, or the very limited attention span of a group of feral five-year-olds may quickly wane.

HEIDI'S HINTS
TIMING IS EVERYTHING

If the main focus of your gathering isn't the food, timing your soirée to begin after dinner is a great way to limit the amount of food you will need to buy and prepare. Everyone will have eaten their main meal at home, leaving you needing to only provide bowls of nibbles instead of a pricey full-blown smorgasbord of munchable delights.

FRUGAL FEASTING

If a feast *is* on the menu, batch cook large one-pot meals. A selection of varied canapés and nibbles will cost way more than a vat of chilli and rice, a curry, jacket potatoes or even slow-cooked pulled pork or beef joints with rolls to make sliders. Switching to veggie options for curries and chillies reduces the cost even further, as the meat is the most expensive component of the meal.

I hosted Christmas dinner this year and it cost me 54p. Yes, that's right, a measly 54p. I waited until a week before the big day and bought the 29p veggies, which are always reduced across all of the supermarkets the week prior to Christmas day. I also bought two large chickens using my Nectar card points. In previous years, I had dutifully bought a large, overpriced turkey – because that's what you do at Christmas. A quick canvass of my guests revealed that no one actually craved turkey – they much preferred a juicy chicken with crispy skin. Turkey is more expensive per kilo than chicken, and I avoided paying through the nose for something that no one particularly liked just because of tradition.

TOP TAKEAWAYS

THRIFTY GIFTS, SPECIAL OCCASIONS & CELEBRATIONS

- Create a party saving pot.
- Create a party budget and stick with it.
- Source preloved gifts, wrapping and decorations whenever you can.
- Get the kids involved in making decorations, wrapping and gifts.
- Try swapping decorations with friends if you want to refresh your theme.
- Share the load by suggesting guests bring a bottle or dish to the party.
- Have fun and improvise – it doesn't have to be perfect and you don't have to spend a lot of money. Your special occasion is about connecting with the people that you love, not how much money you have spent on it.

CHAPTER 10

A STYLISH HOME

When my son was born, I still lived in my one-bedroom party girl flat. I hung up my party shoes and, as I eased into mummydom, my quirky little abode didn't feel like a home for a growing family. I found a rambling four-bedroom terrace in the most deprived area of town – making sure I got the most bang for my buck in terms of square footage – and within seven months of my son being born, we had moved.

My belongings and furniture that had filled my tiny flat with character and style were lost in my new home. I can remember walking into sparsely furnished rooms to a hollow echo. It was minimalism taken to its extreme, and I was itching to make my house a home. I had very limited funds, no idea where to start and a desperate impatience to create a cosy yet beautiful space.

I made some early mistakes on décor, as the task in hand was overwhelming. Back in 2007, there wasn't the volume of internet references for inspiration and ideas, and I admit to resorting to a bit of Swedish flat-pack furniture (hated it!) to fill the rooms with something. My number one tip is to be patient – it takes time to curate a home full of personality, love and style on a budget. My number two tip is to plan – this will help you to hone your radar toward finding affordable treasure that will fit perfectly into your home.

"Be patient – it takes time to curate a home full of personality, love and style on a budget."

Of course, interior trends, tastes and needs change over time, and my home has evolved with both these and my growing family. But the same principles apply: don't rush and plan any changes that you want to make before you jump in with both feet and start making big changes. This chapter is full of hacks and hints to find savvy solutions to create a uniquely stylish home on a shoestring.

PLAN

I am a project manager by day, so I would say, "Plan, plan, and then plan some more." But hear me out. You wouldn't set off on holiday without *any* knowledge of your destination. You would get terribly lost if you did; hell, you wouldn't even be able to coordinate flights and timings, you wouldn't know what to pack and you wouldn't know what currency you needed. The same applies to kitting out and designing your home on a budget. If you do not have a vision or end goal in sight, how can you possibly achieve the vibe that you want? You gotta define that vibe!

If you have multiple rooms to decorate, it's a good idea to decide on a theme, or colour scheme that flows through your home. Having a clear plan throughout creates a sense of calculated consciousness and congruence – it also means that paint can be reused in different rooms, and furnishings, knick-knacks and accessories can be moved around and reused in different spaces when you fancy a change. It is always a thriftier option to reuse what you have already, so when you get the urge to mix things up a little on the interiors front, you can shop from what you have already.

MOOD BOARD IT

To create a plan, draw inspiration from as many mediums as possible: pictures in magazines or books, paint colour cards, nature, Pinterest, Instagram, home décor shops online and on the high street. I have even resorted to snooping through street-level windows and Zoopla for home inspo. The next step is to create a physical scrapbook or mood board; if you prefer a digital option, use a creative app like Canva or Milanote; these allow you to drag and drop images into your design. Focus on pulling together a colour scheme based on your inspiration, as well as focusing on textures, fabrics, ceramics and lighting that work well with your end vision.

Your mood board creates the destination and helps you to plan the steps to get there: what paint to buy, where in your home to paint, what furnishings you need to source, what textures and accessories to look out for. The most important thing to remember is the end result will not be identical to the dream house you covet. On a budget, you will need to make compromises. The mood board will aid you in creating a shopping list of things to look out for and to collect over time. It is all about interpretation rather than copycat, which is why it takes time and patience. The products featured in interiors magazines are often prohibitively expensive; you are aiming to emulate and translate the images into your own affordable version of a style so that it's unique to you and within your budget.

It may sound a bit fancy, but I chose a Nordic Noir theme for my home: black, light grey, unglazed ceramics, dried flowers and stems, wicker, blonde wood and old brass, copper and sheepskin. Although every room is unique, the theme runs through the house. I am not an interior designer, neither am I one to blow my own trumpet, but whenever someone visits my home for the first time, their first words are usually, "Wow! Are you an interior designer? I love your home. Who designed this for you?" The truth is, I have learned from past mistakes and really honed the knack of planning to create a stunning home for next to nothing.

SOURCES

Over the years I have exhausted every source available to find bargain furnishings, paint, knick-knacks and finishing touches for my home. Before you start to curate bits and bobs to create your dream interior, I recommend familiarising yourself with what sources you have available locally. If you can find interiors sources local to you (particularly for bulky items like furniture), it is usually more prudent because it can reduce or even eliminate expensive shipping or delivery costs.

CAR BOOT SALES

Find out where your nearest boot sales are and give it a try. My absolute favourite day of the week is Sunday, when I get to mooch at our local car boot sales. You never know what you will find, and because they are totally random you can often find really quirky and unique pieces for your home. Lurking among other people's junk can be some wonderful hidden gems. For the most part, I will never pay more than a fiver for something from a boot sale, and my preferred threshold is £2. You can haggle, especially if you are buying a few bits from a seller. But if you see something that you like, snap it up – at a boot sale there is no time for faffing or indecisiveness, as it won't be there if you change your mind and go back. Some of my most recent car-boot finds have been Anthropologie cushions, French copper bowls, a seventies German pottery jug, an original seventies peacock chair and a Dartmouth Pottery glug fish jug.

CHARITY SHOPS

Charity shops are a great source for home accessories such as curtains, cushions, vases, jugs, ceramics, glasses and kitchen utensils, and much, much more. While slightly more expensive than car boot sales, you can still pick up items at a fraction of their original retail price. Larger charities often have superstores where they sell furnishings and offer local delivery at a reasonable rate. Locally, we have a charity warehouse that sells factory second unused mattresses at a fifth of the recommended retail price! It's definitely worth researching whether any of your local shops carry seconds or deadstock for essential home items like this.

I do find that charity shops can be pricey for quality items. Ultimately, they are there to make money for the charity, so – particularly with the larger, national or international charities – staff often research manufacturers' marks and labels to get an inkling of price point. As a result, any high-quality, designer or antique items will be sold online, which reduces your chance of finding a breathtaking find for a few quid. That said, good fortune and the charity shop gods may shine on you, and you may just find that killer item that has slipped through the net.

HOUSE CLEARANCE AUCTIONS & JUNK SHOPS

General house clearances are generally from deceased estates, and are an absolute treasure trove of quirky vintage finds. If you are lucky enough to have a regular general house clearance auction in your town or city, I would highly recommend giving it a whirl, at least once. It can be daunting at first if you never have attended an auction before. My first time was fraught with nerves, and I got stage fright about sticking my hand in the air: What if I scratch my nose by accident, will I end up shelling out hundreds on a rickety armoire? What if I really want something and someone bids against me? What do I do? Just relax and enjoy it. They really are informal, and filled with a mix of local wheeler-dealer characters, hustlers and middle-class upcycling mums sourcing for their furniture renovation micro-businesses.

Once you commit to an item, set a budget so that you don't get caught up in a bidding frenzy. There is usually a pre-auction online catalogue available prior to the auction and literally anything can pop up for sale: plant pots, vintage salt and pepper shakers, full dinner services and lots of wooden furniture. I have found so many teak mid-century sideboards, bureaus and chairs, along with Sputnik-era curtain fabric, vintage sewing boxes full of the original owner's sewing kit, and vintage lace and thread from the 1960s. None of the items that I have ever bought sold for more than £10, as that was my limit. I did resell some of the teak furniture, deciding it was too much in my home. My best resale was a mid-century Jentique bureau that I sold for £485 on eBay.

Alternatively, if you don't have the mettle to face an auction experience, look out for house clearance shops – and don't be afraid to haggle.

SCRANNYING (OR LANING) & SKIP DIVING

"Scrannying" is something I have done for years. I didn't even know that it had a name until I worked on a project with colleagues in our local refuse collection team. We were talking about fly tipping, and I explained how my friend and I liked to drive around streets and back lanes inspecting fly tips for treasure. Unbeknown to me, we had a name; we were scranniers. If you live in a student town, this is particularly prevalent at the end of term when youngsters clear out their digs, and fly tip chairs, desks, storage and decorative bits and pieces. The more socially conscious ones will list on free sites, but there are plenty of goodies fly tipped in back lanes and in front of houses. I always drive around with one eye open for dumped treasure that I can repurpose. I have found full dinner sets, tables and chairs, vintage sewing machine tables and exercise equipment, as well as toys and games.

Skips can also be a good source of treasure. If I see a skip parked outside a house and can see chair legs peeking out, I will have a snoop. Always knock on the door first and ask permission before poking around on someone's private property, and ask if they are happy for you to take anything they don't want. I have found unearthed sideboards, skateboards and half-used tins of paint in skips. When you are speaking to the homeowner, always check if there is anything sharp or corrosive that you need to know about in the skip before you start hoisting treasure out. You don't want to get injured on your quest for a freebie.

TIPS & RECYCLING CENTRES

Visit your nearest Tip Shop or Reuse Shop, which are usually located at your local recycling centre. You can feel incredibly virtuous that you are doing your bit for the environment and literally saving something that was destined for landfill or incineration. Staff at your local recycling centre are trained to spot and pick out saleable items which then become stock for the Tip Shop – this could be anything from tins of paint to furniture, toys, bric-a-brac and home accessories. It is really random, but prices are low. The same principle applies to the Tip Shop as it does to auctions and car boot sales: you have to train your eye to look beyond the junk and pick out pieces that fit with your mood board and vision.

"Train your eye to look beyond the junk."

FREEBIES

There is only one thing better than a bargain, getting something for free. As well as being kind on your pocket, you are doing someone a favour by taking their unwanted clutter away – one man's trash and all that. There are a multitude of websites and apps where people can post their "free to a good home" items. Register with Freecycle, Olio, Freegle and local Don't Dump It groups on Facebook. A regular search for £0 or FREE on Gumtree and Facebook Marketplace should bring up freebies too. A word of caution: you need to be quick; people like free stuff and the better items get snapped up. Equally, if you are having a spring clean and want to get rid of stuff in double-quick time, list it on free groups and give your own unwanted things a new home.

ONLINE SOURCES

Facebook Marketplace and Gumtree are well established virtual local boot sales. Marketplace is probably the first place I look if I need a piece of furniture or extra finishing touches for my home. You can set up alerts for items, you can haggle, you can collect quickly, and – most importantly – you can grab a bargain. Browsing Marketplace for treasure is my number two sport, after car booting.

My most ridiculous find was listed as a chair and footstool for £20. It was in a quiet hamlet 30 miles away in one of those big country houses that you wistfully dream about while browsing Zoopla. On closer inspection, it was an original vintage Knoll Mies van der Rohe Barcelona chair and footstool, listed online at over £6,000. I have never driven so fast in my life, coursing down country lanes at breakneck speed with no idea how I was going to cram it into my Nissan Micra. It was coming home with me even if I had to carry it back down the motorway. Often people don't actually know what they have got, particularly if they have inherited it or been gifted it. The trick is to not be too specific in searches, as listing titles that don't reference a particular brand, era, or the terms "retro" or "vintage", are more likely to yield an absolute steal.

HEIDI'S HINTS
THE POWER OF GOOGLE LENS

I highly recommend using Google Lens to search for dupes if there is something you have seen in a magazine or on Pinterest and absolutely fallen in love with. For example, I recently found some architectural concrete artichokes on the Liberty London website retailing at £415 each; a quick search with Google Lens uncovered something almost exactly the same for just £5 at The Range. The items look identical and serve exactly the same purpose, so why buy the overpriced ones? Who are you trying to impress? I honestly believe it's way more impressive to have found a budget designer dupe than to have shelled out an exorbitant amount of money for house knick-knacks. Impress people with your savvy shopping rather than your snobbery; I guarantee they will be asking for tips and pointers on how to grab a designer piece for pennies.

UPCYCLING

Just because a piece of furniture is a bog-standard MDF flat pack eyesore or a water-stained and scratched wooden monstrosity, doesn't mean it has to stay that way. Picture frames, lamp bases, vases, plant pots are also all fair game to be revamped to fit in with your design scheme. The mantra that apples to thrifted clothes also applies to preloved home décor and furniture – just because an item presents a certain way, doesn't mean it has to stay that way. It is all about the art of the possible,and you have to train your eye to see the hidden potential when you are sourcing.

There are many furniture paint formulations on the market that require little preparation to get great results: chalk paint, milk paint, mineral paint. My particular favourite is Fusion Mineral Paint: it dries quickly, gives fabulous cover, is waterproof, adheres to literally anything and needs no waxing or sealing. I am a slapdash and impatient upcycler – I know what I want to achieve and want it now. I don't have the time, inclination or patience to sand, undercoat and wait hours between coats.

I recommend practising on small piece of furniture or a picture frame first, so that you get used to handling the paint, but it really is idiot-proof (take it from me!). Picture frames and lamp bases are a great, cheap way to update a colour scheme or tie a piece in with your vision. You can even paint traditional, old-fashioned ornaments to create a quirky, funky objet d'art.

There are lots of upcycling tutorials on YouTube and inspiration on Pinterest. To really bring a revamped piece of furniture to life, change the handles for something a bit fancier. A quick search on eBay for vintage handles brings up a huge amount of choice that will put the perfect finishing touch to your masterpiece.

DECORATING

The cheapest way to update a tired home is to give it a lick of paint. After a few years of general living, cats, kids and various trips and slips with drinks in hand, my house starts to look in need of a refresh. I also get bored of looking at exactly the same room for years on end. Nothing kicks me into action like the blossoming of spring or the autumnal cocooning mood. These are the times when I usually feel inspired to switch things up a bit.

However, paint is expensive – and fancy paint is *insanely* pricey. Brands like Farrow & Ball, Abigail Ahern and Lick do those lush, muted fashionable colours with cool (albeit sometimes ridiculous) names, but, at the end of the day, it's just paint. If I find a paint I like from one of the fancy brands, I take the colour swatch to my local Brewers or Johnstone's decorating centre and they mix the paint to the exact colour for a fraction of the price; and, in my opinion, the trade paint offers much better coverage and quality.

You can get specialist paints to cover most surfaces (Rust-Oleum and Ronseal do great ranges). If your kitchen cabinets or tiles are looking a bit sorry for themselves, a lick of paint can completely transform you kitchen or bathroom. Whether it be wood, metal, plastic or tile, a lot of modern specialist paint formulations will transform and uplift a tired room. Dismayed by my grotty UPVC windows, I recently discovered the holy grail of "stick to anything" waterproof paint, Zinsser Allcoat. This little tub of magic completely refreshed my grotty, yellowing UPVC window frames; it could also be used for a walk-in shower surround. Have you been eyeing up one of those lovely brightly coloured composite front doors? Save yourself a fortune by not buying the door and just using Zinsser paint to give your home instant kerb appeal.

Your local Tip Shop is also worth a visit for paint. How many times have you had to buy an extra tin to finish off a job? You may, like me, be prudent and keep the tin for touch-ups. However, not everyone is thrifty, and will load up the car for a tip run laden with decorating debris, often including barely dipped into tins of paint. If you like a sludgy muted tone, why not try mixing a few together (just make sure that you have enough overall to finish the job!).

If you are really strapped for cash, try just painting a single statement wall. A chimney breast or the wall opposite a bright window works well. This reduces the amount of paint that you need so automatically costs far less.

Wallpapering a statement wall with a mural or wallpaper is also a great way to lift a space, but the higher end wallpapers and murals cost a bomb. I found some gorgeous wallpaper with a chinoiserie heron print online; it was by Gucci and cost a whopping £415 a roll. After a quick Google Lens search, I had found a dupe on Etsy for £32 a roll. I used the leftovers to line drawers, and even framed a segment to create a picture to go on the opposite wall to tie the theme in. Google Lens is great for sniffing out more affordable versions of designer wallpapers.

NO-COST ROOM MAKEOVERS

My favourite thing to do is completely overhaul a room with zero or very minimal budget. It does take slightly longer to revamp a room if you have no budget whatsoever, as you need to be patient while selling off the existing decorative items and furnishings, but it's worth it to have a net-zero financial and environmental impact. There are stages to achieving a no-/low-cost total room makeover.

- Create your mood board theme or vision for the room.
- Decide what existing pieces from the room will work with your theme and keep them.
- List unwanted items on Facebook Marketplace, Gumtree or eBay (don't be too ambitious on pricing, you want them gone and the cash in your pocket. I always list for £5 more than I would like, so if someone makes me a lower offer I'm

happy to accept it and they think they've got a bargain!) Sell anything, don't underestimate what people will buy. I literally sold a piece of old rope just to satisfy myself that I could get money for old rope! Cushions, duvet sets. Toys, pictures, mirrors, rugs, decorative bits, candles, plants sell them all.

- Make a shopping list of the things you need to bring your new room vision to life (remember it's all about improvising and getting the closest that you can to the products on your mood board).

- If you are repainting, you will want to buy your paint first as that is the canvas for all of your other bargain finds.

- Now, the fun bit: collecting preloved goodies off Marketplace, Gumtree, car boot sales and charity shops to fill your redesigned space. Using the money from the sales of the bits that no longer fit with your grand design, you are aiming to come in at net-zero pounds. Make cheeky offers when you can, see the upcycling potential and beauty in items and be patient. Curating a room for nothing can take a little longer, but it's absolutely worth it. Set Marketplace alerts if you are looking for a particular thing, so you can be responsive – bargains are snapped up at lightspeed.

- Put a call-out on free sites, as someone may be looking to get rid of something similar to what you are looking for.

- Once you have restyled the room, take a step back and reassess what else it might need – the finishing touches that would elevate your new room and make it perfect. Make a mental note of the items you think are missing and take your time to curate the final little details (at a bargain price, of course).

THE GARDEN & OUTDOOR SPACES

I am a huge advocate for shopping out of season, whether it be for preloved or brand new items. If you live in the UK, summer is very short-lived and demand for both used and shop-bought al fresco-themed goodies drives prices up exactly when you need them most. I circle like a shark for out-of-season bargains, whether it be garden furniture and barbecues or swimwear and snuggly coats.

The best garden or outdoor space bargains are to be had at the end of September through to the beginning of October. Everyone has given up on the annual promise of an Indian summer and decided to either defeatedly pack away their garden furniture, outdoor rugs, cushions, lights and barbecues for the year or to sell them on, vowing to buy new the next year. Meanwhile, retailers are desperate to make room for Christmas displays and slash the prices of the last dregs of the summer sales. This is when I pounce to snap up summer bargains.

If you are unable to store garden furniture or accessories over winter, don't despair as there is another great time to snap up preloved outdoor goodies, but you will need to be quick off the mark. The first glimmer of spring, around April, has ashen-faced Brits sleepily emerging from winter hibernation and inspecting their gardens properly for the first time since autumn. They survey, scratch their chins and descend on B&Q and Homebase en masse to replace tired garden furniture with shiny new products for their picture-perfect gardens. Where do they offload the unwanted stuff? Facebook Marketplace, of course! Preloved garden and outdoors listings hit a peak in April and May, but beware: everyone is looking for a bargain, so you snooze, you lose. Hover over Marketplace on your smartphone, set up alerts, and check in every couple of hours to grab a bargain for your outdoor space.

"Preloved garden and outdoors listings hit a peak in April and May."

Some of my best garden bargains have been plants bought out of season. I fund a huge Torbay palm tree for £50 in a local garden centre in October; it had seen better days, but I knew that with some TLC I could nurse it back to life – and it was worth a bit of effort for the whopping £300 saving that I made. DIY superstores and garden centres only have so much space, and heavily reduce seasonal outdoor plants once the nights draw in. When summer has peaked and pumpkin-themed décor, snacks and drinks start to appear on shelves, perennials, shrubs and trees start to look a bit tired, lose their leaves and shrivel – none of which is very appealing to shoppers. This is the time to stock up on plants, heavily reduced and looking a bit beyond their best. Come spring, as the Earth tilts on its axis, your shabby, bargain plants will be reinvigorated by sunlight and April showers and become as good as new.

TOP TAKEAWAYS
A STYLISH HOME

- Have a plan and a vision for the style you want to create.
- Research local sources for preloved and free furniture and homeware.
- Use Google Lens to look for dupes of expensive designer homeware and wallcoverings.
- Take colour swatches from high-end paint collections to your local trade centre for colour matching and mixing at a fraction of the price.
- Makeover a room with zero budget by selling unwanted stuff and using the proceeds to buy the new (preloved) stuff.
- Try shopping out of season for garden and outdoor spaces.

CHAPTER 11

BARGAIN DAYS OUT & JOYFUL MOMENTS

Even on the tightest of budgets you need to be able to carve out some space for fun – to do things that bring you and your family joy. Life would be unbearable if all you did was count pennies and deny yourself any pleasure whatsoever. You quite literally cannot pour from an empty cup, meaning if your resilience and spirit is depleted, you won't have anything left to offer your family, friends, employer and – most importantly – yourself.

Tightening your belt and budgeting doesn't mean denying yourself everything. Before I knew better, I would often start a (doomed) Monday fad diet, you know the ones: no carbs, no sugar, 1,500 calories, no meals after 6pm, the list goes on. I would stick to it for a few days; on Day One I would follow the diet fastidiously, go to bed with my belly rumbling but feeling smug. I would wake up feeling like a supermodel, like I'd lost a stone overnight, albeit with a growling tummy. I would usually last until teatime on Day Two, consumed with thoughts of Pringles, baguette, cheese and pastry. By then, I convinced myself I had done well enough to deserve a treat, only to go into a feeding frenzy, munching through the contents of the fridge like the Hungry Caterpillar.

It's not that diets don't work, but restricting and denying yourself completely will leave you craving the thing you are denying yourself, and ultimately lead to binging and overconsumption. The same principle applies to money. If you deny yourself any pleasure whatsoever, you are way more likely to have "stuff it" moments and overspend. So, how do you overcome the vicious cycle of self-denial and splurging?

"If you deny yourself any pleasure whatsoever, you are way more likely to have "stuff it" moments and overspend."

When the kids were little, before they became backchatting teens who think I am tragic, I would allocate all of my fun budget on activities with them, making memories. We were on a single income and there was scant disposable income, so not all of these activities cost money, but I did budget for fuel to get places. Over the years, I have tried every hustle and hack to get free and cheap days out for the family. Even now with my teenagers (who can occasionally be lured to grace me with their company if it involves food), I use discounts and hacks to find cheap eats and fun things that we can do together – having adventures together builds and maintains relationships and creates new memories. You don't need a mega-budget to let some light in, as there are lots of things that you can do for free.

THE BEST THINGS IN LIFE ARE FREE

The things that I consider fun would have other people running for the hills. Rummaging through piles of other people's old

232

clothes and junk at a car boot sale, lifting weights, baking in the sun like a lizard on a sandy Devon beach. Everyone's idea of fun is subjective, and how we spend our leisure time is unique to us.

The ideas below are in no way exhaustive as they are based on things that *I* have done for fun. You might read this section and think, "Umm, those things don't sound like fun to me," and you will be bang on – everyone finds enjoyment in different things. Mind you, some of these activities didn't sound appealing to me until I tried them. On a tiny budget, I have always had to be open-minded about doing new things if they are free. What is the worst that can happen?

PICNICS

You eat dinner anyway, so transport it outdoors, somewhere with a nice view preferably. Nothing beats packing up a budget dinner and eating outside. When the clocks have gone back and the evenings are light, I like to have evening barbecues on the beach or in the park; the kids can bring friends and you are all out in the fresh air away from home. Battling with sausages rolling off a disposable barbie and picking bits of grass off a rogue burger is all part of the fun. For the cost of some buns and burgers you have a fun evening out.

GET OUTSIDE

One of the best feelings in the world is coming home, kicking off your shoes and relaxing with a brew. But you can't enjoy this feeling unless you get out of the house first of all. Either with your kids, with friends or on your own, get out for a walk – it's free. If I don't have money for fuel, I like to walk locally, but make it a mission to take photographs of five things I haven't really noticed the beauty in before. It's one thing stomping along in the rain, head down, hood up because the dog needs a poo, to mindfully walking along looking for things you hadn't noticed before – a gargoyle on the top of a church, a spider's web on a street sign, a blue plaque that had never caught your eye before, sunlight bouncing off the windows of a high rise. Looking for beauty on well-trodden paths really makes you stop and enjoy what you have on your doorstep. Getting the kids involved in finding five special things to take photographs of when they are walking with you is great for their creativity and, best of all, it is free. You could start a blog of your photographs to encourage them to join in curating these moments of beauty right on your doorstep.

In lockdown, my bestie, Kay, and I, would go for sunrise walks. We would mooch along at 5.30am, when the roads and city were peaceful and shrouded in golden light, and we would explore undiscovered nooks, streets and gardens. Our early morning strolls lifted our spirits and brought us an absolute joy that we still talk about today. Night walks, morning walks, dusk walks, frosty walks, rainy walks are all great ways to quite literally see your local area in a new light – and nothing beats the feeling of getting home and kicking off your walking shoes after an invigorating wander. Get out – whatever the weather!

GET LOST

The best free days out I have ever had are those where we got lost. The most memorable being a walk around Glen Affric on the wettest day imaginable. We had walked for miles without getting anywhere nearer to the car park, so made the decision to find our way back by crossing over a shallow stretch of water. It wasn't a sensible decision: it was deeper than we expected, slippery, and we ended up even wetter with my mum (no spring chicken) sliding down a mossy rock and ending up chest deep in freezing water. It was all a bit perilous, but we were howling with laughter at our predicament. Even though it felt a teeny bit hellish at the time, we all look back at the adventure as one of our fondest memories.

I like to do magical mystery tours; all it costs is half a tank of fuel. We bundle in the car with snacks and drive with no definite destination in mind. The kids have no idea where we are going, and I have no clear plan either. We simply drive out into the countryside, find somewhere to park and explore a new place. We don't know what will be at the end of the journey, but creating an adventure together creates memories that stay. We have discovered huge rocks to climb, reservoirs and lakes, old graveyards and churches, rogue sheep and ponies. Even if you need the reassurance of knowing where you are and secretly peek at the satnav, the thrill of the unknown is a great adventure for kids, regardless of their age.

LETTERBOXING & GEOCACHING

If you really want to pimp up your walks, letterboxing and geocaching are a great way to give the outing a purpose.

Letterboxing involves weatherproof boxes containing clues to other boxes. There is usually a notebook in the box where you can sign in and write a note for others to read – serious letterboxers detail their find count.

Similarly, geocaching mixes treasure hunting with orienteering. You use your phone GPS to look for hidden treasure. You can register at geocaching.com, set up an account and get started. Again, it's great because it creates a mission for your walk and gets you exploring places that you might not have visited before.

MUSEUMS & ART GALLERIES

The majority of UK museums and art galleries are free. When the children were small, I took them with trepidation to our local museum. It was raining and they were driving me potty indoors, so off we trooped, in search of a change of scenery to break the sibling tension. I thought they would be bored; I didn't think that dusty relics and historical paintings would capture their interest. How wrong I was – they loved it! They had learned about Sir Francis Drake in school, and were excited to see paintings of ships and explorers. They loved looking at the display cases – fossils and jars of preserved animal remains lined up like jars in a sweet shop. It was magical to them, and it was absolutely free. Of course, you need to bring the magic to life and engage them, but once you get a hook in they are captivated.

More recently, I visited a travelling art exhibition. It was billed as an immersive experience and, I will be totally honest, thought it would be high-brow, snooty and up its own backside. Again, I was proved so wrong. One exhibit required me to sit on a bench in a white room, in front of jars, jugs, kettles and other household objects (even slow cookers and saucepans); the objects were set up with microphones and each receptacle played a note (like a yoga singing bowl). Well, being in this simple space, sitting still and listening to the eerie sounds made me well up with tears. I kid you not, it made me feel incredibly emotional. I can't tell you why, and I wasn't expecting it, but I felt wonderful when I came out.

Even if you think you wouldn't enjoy a free museum or art gallery, give it a go. You might be pleasantly surprised.

A SONG & A DANCE

When both the weather and finances are dismal, singing and dancing (albeit behind closed curtains) is a great way to let off steam with kids – or on your own. There are tons of dance tutorials on YouTube, and having a living room dance-off is a great way to have a giggle, get a bit of exercise in and get the whole family, or your pals, being silly. Of course, there are games consoles that will let you keep score on dances – and that's great if you have one already. Similarly, we would cast the kids' favourite music videos from YouTube to the TV and they would dance and sing like they were auditioning for *The X Factor*. This would keep them entertained for hours and tire them out for bed, which is always a bonus.

One of the best birthday gifts my daughter received was a karaoke microphone. That beloved bit of £15 plastic tat bought many hours of family fun and laughter. We would take it in turns to belt out chart-topping hits in comedic tones. I'm not sure whether the neighbours were as keen, but the unbridled joy of singing badly at the top of our lungs bought us many hours of laughs – and hoarse throats.

GAME NIGHT

Take it in turns with friends to host a Game Night. Pull out Cards Against Humanity, Pictionary, Charades, Twister, Monopoly, or whatever games you have to hand and that are age-appropriate. When my two children were small and they got restless indoors on long rainy days, I always found that it broke the boredom and any tension by counterintuitively inviting more kids into the mix. Hosting an impromptu games afternoon with friends was a great way to keep them occupied, even if it was party games like Simon Says. As an adult, I have hosted Monopoly nights, but it comes with a warning: hyper-competitive types may just reveal their true colours, and there has been the occasional fall out over Park Lane.

"Spending time with good friends is food for the soul."

BUDDY UP FOR DATE NIGHTS

Date nights are not just about romance. As adults, it's so easy to get wrapped up in the treadmill of work and, before you know it, a few months have passed since you spent quality time with good friends. Organising a regular friend date night is a great way to carve out space for each other, and share the effort and cost of cooking. My bestie and I have twice-weekly date nights: the kids and I all pile to hers on a Tuesday for dinner, they come back to ours on Thursdays. This means we both have a night off cooking and dishes, and what's the point of us both using up energy and cooking every night when we can share the load a bit. The kids get to catch up, while we eat and gossip and laugh (usually at ourselves). Spending time with good friends is food for the soul, and if you are rubbish at staying in touch, planning a weekly, fortnightly, monthly evening makes sure that you make time to catch up and have fun.

BOOK CLUBS & LIBRARIES

If you love reading and feel bereft when you have finished a great book, you can keep it alive by sharing your feeling and thoughts on the book by joining a book club. You don't even need to buy the book, you can borrow it from your local library; if it's not in stock and it's a new title, ask the librarian to transfer a copy from a neighbouring library or order one in for you. The library is also a good starting point to find a local book club – look on community notice boards. Facebook community groups are also a great way to find local activities like book clubs, or you could start one with work colleagues or friends. If you prefer to share your reading experience online, there are lots of online book clubs where you can review books and connect with other book lovers. My favourites are the National Centre for Writing and Belletrist, or you could check out Between Two Books and Reese's Book Club, among others.

COMMUNITY DAYS OUT

Never one to pass up a freebie, I like to keep a keen eye on my local council's "What's On" page on their website. I live in Plymouth, and we have an online calendar of free events… pirate days, fêtes and festivals, Armed Forces events, firework displays, trails and walks, and food fairs. I tend to avoid the food events with kids in tow as their overall aim is to part you from your cash; while entry is free and you do get to test and taste small samples, the food costs money and the kids will badger – it's no longer a free day out if you have bought two hot dogs for £16. Sign up for local authority "What's on" alerts for free stuff to do on your doorstep.

LITTER PICKS & BEACH CLEANS

Maybe gathering the detritus flung out of passing car windows or clearing the carnage left by irresponsible picnickers isn't your idea of fun, but being part of a group, getting out into the community and having a real sense of purpose and achievement are all great ways to have fun and boost your mood while giving back at the same time. My children loved to get involved in beach and park cleans when they were small; as well as getting them out in the fresh air, it instilled good habits and values around littering in them. I recommend joining an organised group that provides safety vests, litter grabbers and council-issued bin bags. Facebook community groups are a great resource to find a local group to join, or look on your local council website for volunteer groups.

ALLOCATE A FUN BUDGET

I am all in favour of making the most of free days out, but what if the well of free runs dry, or you want to do something that involves eating out, or you want to venture to new pastures? This is where the fun budget comes into its own.

In the same way that we discussed planning menus and shopping lists based on a grocery budget, I like to plan outings and activities based around money allocated to the fun budget. This could be a cinema trip, a woodland walk on a damp day, a budget dinner out or a regular club or membership. The point is to build doing things that make you feel happy into your overall budget, even if this is just for the fuel or bus fare to get you somewhere that makes you happy.

Prioritising doing things just for enjoyment, even if you are strapped for cash, is vital as it releases happy chemicals in the brain that make you feel more positive and reduce stress. It's so easy to get bogged down in misery and self-pity when you are juggling a meagre budget, but taking time out for play will absolutely boost your mood and give you the resilience you need to feel in control and see positive opportunities to live well for less.

The fun budget covers extra fuel, dinners out, entrance fees, food, anything related to the things you do for fun.

GET ORGANISED

You're going to want to make the most of your fun budget by searching out discounts and savings wherever you can. Make yourself a plan, and schedule in some free and some paid-for activities, working out what you can do with your fun budget.

My month's fun budget is £80: £54 for activities and the remainder for petrol to get places. You need to remember to budget for travel cards, bus passes or coach fares if you are using public transport. Below is a typical four-week plan for my family.

Week	Monday	Tuesday	Wednesday	Thursday	Friday	Saturday	Sunday
1		Bestie Date Night			Bestie Date Night	Game Night	Car boot £15
2	Online escape room £5	Bestie Date Night	Cinema for four £14		Bestie Date Night	Prezzo pizza night out for four £20	Woodland walk
3		Bestie Date Night		Book Club catch up	Bestie Date Night	Coastal path walk and picnic	Dartmoor Letterboxing
4		Bestie Date Night	Beach picnic barbecue		Bestie Date Night	Monthly date with pals	Beach walk

Getting bargain activities does require you to download a few apps and sign up for offers, but it will be worth it – I promise.

MEERKAT MOVIES & MEALS

I cannot recall a year when I didn't use the Meerkat (Compare the Market) offers to save money on the cinema and on restaurants locally. The only catch is that you have to purchase an insurance product from Compare the Market to get access to the discounts. If you don't need insurance, no problem – I buy a one-day single trip travel insurance policy for an imaginary day out in London, with a high voluntary excess to ensure the lowest price. The premium comes in at around £1, which opens the door to a year of Meerkat discounts: BOGOF Movies on Tuesdays and Wednesdays and discounted meals; Prezzo is our go-to for meals as it's also BOGOF.

MEAL DEALS

OK, they may not serve up Michelin-starred fodder, but chain pubs and restaurants regularly offer discounts and freebies. These can range from Kids Eat Free deals to Birthday freebies and extra menu items. One way to access half-price meals for a limited period is to sign up for a TasteCard 60-day trial for £1 (the card also offers cinema and attraction discounts). Just set a diary note on day 59, along with the password and email you used to sign up, to ensure that you cancel before the trial period ends. It's handy to sign up to this just before the school summer holidays start. It's a bit cheeky, but when your 60-day trial has expired, you could get someone else in the house to sign up for another 60 days for £1.

I recommend taking an inventory of the chain pubs and restaurants in your local area that are likely to have websites or apps (e.g.

Greene King, Table Table, Beefeater, Brewers Fayre), and research deals. They do change all the time, but current offers that I found while writing this section were BOGOF burgers, kids' free breakfasts, 25% off whole order, and two main courses for £11. Similarly, chains like Frankie & Benny's, TGI Fridays, Nando's, Turtle Bay, YO! Sushi, Wildwood, Pho, Bella Italia and Hub Box all have offers and discounts if you sign up online. These range from dinner and cinema bundles, Kids Eat Free (school holidays), a free whole chicken, free drinks, 20% discount, two courses for £10, NHS, Military and student discounts, free main course just for signing up, kids eat for £1, etc.

When you are planning what you are going to do with your fun budget, *never* step foot in a café or restaurant without checking out the offers online first. If you couldn't find anything, call the restaurant and ask; plus I always check the offer is still available before we are seated (as you can imagine, my kids are mortified and try to disown me). Very often there will be exclusive app-based discounts on top of website promotions, so making sure that you do your due diligence first ensures that you get as much bang for your buck as possible. A large percentage of these retailers offer free kids' meals in the school holidays, so they are a great way of having a treat for a fraction of the price.

NATIONAL TRUST

The most useful membership I have ever had for days out has been with the trusty National Trust. Monthly memberships are reasonable and, as well as giving you access to stunning properties and gardens, fairs and seasonal events, it gives you free parking at beaches, woodland and other AONB sites. Some of our fondest family memories have been made on National Trust days out: bank holiday Punch and Judy shows on the lawn in front of Killerton House; dressing up as Victorian children in Buckland Abbey; visiting Christmas illuminations and drinking hot chocolate outdoors wrapped up in blankets at Saltram House; and long heady summer days at South Milton Sands. The cost per visit when the kids were little was negligible, and if we were taking advantage of a discounted UK holiday (the *Sun* £10 Cornwall caravan holiday anyone?), we would always plan our holiday around National Trust days out.

SEASON TICKETS & LOCAL PASSES

If you are lucky enough to have attractions such as aquariums, zoos, theme parks or gorgeous gardens on your doorstep, check out whether they have free or discounted passes for locals before making your first visit. At some places, the annual pass can cost more or less the same amount as a single visit and you can bag yourself a year's worth of days out. When the kids were tiny, we barely had any spare cash once the essential bills were paid, and these passes were a lifesaver. We absolutely maxxed out the National Marine Aquarium and Crealy Theme Park memberships. The combined total of all of these, including the National Trust subscription was £50 a month, but there wasn't a weekend that went by where we didn't use all or some of these passes to make memories and have fun together.

WILD(ISH) CAMPING

Some of my best (almost) free days out have been wildish camping. I say almost free as the owner of the field with compost toilet and an outdoor cold water shower charges us £10 for the night. Admittedly, I would only do this myself on gloriously sunny days because I am a bit of a wimp. I would set off with a single-skin pop-up beach tent (we couldn't afford a proper one), two kids and a duvet to set up camp. The kids got filthy, climbed trees and threw things on a fire; we slept with the tent open and star-gazed; we ate quick-cook tortellini and croissants and drank instant coffee in the morning. I swear that's the best coffee I have ever tasted, watching the sun rise over the South Hams on a hot sunny morning, surrounded by cow pats and midges, with grubby but content children snoring gently in a ridiculously inappropriate tent. A random night under the stars really is the best cheap fun adventure.

CITY BREAKS

Living on a small (sometimes soggy) island we are fortunate that we don't have to travel far to take in new towns, cities and scenery. A budget overnight stay makes it even more of an adventure, as a treat doesn't have to cost the earth.

> ## "Exploring somewhere new on foot is a great, free way of discovering hidden gems."

Wowcher and Groupon are great for finding bargain accommodation and city breaks, but do check on other travel sites, such as Trivago and Kayak, to make sure that it really is the best deal. Research your destination and look for free things to do in the local area. If you have National Trust membership, look for local properties to visit, google galleries, museums and "What's On" locally – make yourself a free visit itinerary. Exploring somewhere new on foot (and, again, getting slightly lost) is a great way of discovering hidden gems; being off the beaten track all adds to the adventure. If you are serious about a city break on a budget and don't want to pay for more than one meal out, take some top-up snacks that you can make in your room with hot water: instant oats, ramen noodles, pasta or rice pots, or tortellini. None of these require a fridge, and all can be whipped up using nothing more than a kettle of boiling water, saving you more than a few pennies on extra snacks and meals out.

TOP TAKEAWAYS
BARGAIN DAYS OUT & JOYFUL MOMENTS

- Prioritise play and fun for your wellbeing, whatever your age.
- Create a "fun budget" when you are working out your monthly budget.
- Create a monthly planner of fun things to do that are either free or within your budget.
- Be open minded and try something new.
- Sign up for alerts from local "What's On" and events groups or your local council.
- Research local and annual passes for local attractions.
- Get outside – look for things that you hadn't noticed on your doorstep.
- Register for offers and discounts from local restaurants and cafés.
- Always research online for the cheapest deal and check that the offer is still valid before you eat or stay anywhere.

THRIFTING IS FOR LIFE

I wrote this book with a genuine desire to help people – people just like me, strangled by the cost of living price rises, anxiously lying awake at night fretting about how they will cope with escalating energy and food prices and the ever-looming threat of catastrophic interest rates inflating mortgage and rent payments.

"There is a solution to every problem if you have the right mindset to face it head on."

I found a way through by using my professional and personal skills. I am not a money guru; I can't tell you how best to invest your money or about things like ISAs. I am a planner and an organiser by trade, with a lifelong penchant for thrifty living. What I can help you with is how to create a plan to live well for less, and how to relish the challenge of spotting opportunities to thrift your life.

BEST BEFORE... NEVER

Looking for opportunities to save money, budgeting and cutting your cloth has no end date. Life changes are inevitable, and sometimes your life can change immeasurably – sometimes in the space of a day.

You do not set off on a certain course and remain there steadfastly, heading toward twilight years. You may inherit a large fortune, win the lottery or make millions through fantastic investments and business ideas. Or, it is more likely that you'll be living comfortably until a life event knocks you off kilter: redundancy, maternity, sickness, bereavement, divorce, relocation, study. There are so many situations that can influence our life's course that sometimes our trajectory is forced to change.

When I started writing this book, I was one part of a two-parent household, dual income and two kids. I am now writing my final chapter and am one month into being a single parent. There were many cracks in the relationship, but a chain of events, completely unforeseen, exacerbated the situation and accelerated the separation. I am now, in my 50s, dealing with a huge personal life change that, among other things, has had a major impact on my living budget.

I could have spent every day feeling sorry for myself, feeling like a victim. Instead, I dusted myself off, gave myself a shake and looked for opportunity. Self-pity is self-perpetuating, and as soon as you fall into the trap of feeling like a victim you stifle creative and critical thinking, you miss breaks and chances to improve your own situation. No one is coming to rescue you. It is all down to you to control those things that are controllable. With two children dependent on me, there was no time for giving up or wallowing. Having a positive "can do" mindset has been essential for me to have the strength and energy to hustle, juggle and reorganise the family finances. Had I allowed myself to linger too long on my pity pot, it would have become all-consuming and would have eaten away at my resilience. You really do become what you think, and I refuse to be a victim of circumstance.

> **"Even if you only take away two or three practical tips, I guarantee that you will save money and start to see opportunities to live for less."**

So, what did I do? I went back to the beginning of course! I revisited my budget health check, I looked for different ways to shop for everything that we consume as a smaller family, I analysed my energy usage again. In short, I followed the steps that I have laid out in this book to ensure that we could manage as a family on a drastically reduced monthly budget. I clawed back more money from our budget and, as lean as it is, I found a way to make it work within my means.

BE PREPARED

I have included some blank planning tables that you can copy and use to plan your own budgets. I would recommend making copies of the blank versions, as when things inevitably change you will need to take stock again. If energy prices rise, or (fingers crossed) they fall, it's good practice to know exactly what your appliances cost to run. If you are faced with unforeseen costs or changes in circumstance that leave your budget stretched so thin that things feel impossible, go back to your health check and look for places to flex your costs. If food costs continue to escalate, you may need to revisit your meal planning. Giving yourself visibility and control when faced with anxiety-inducing and seemingly unsurmountable financial challenges will put you on the front foot and help you to see the wood for the trees.

FOR ALL & FOR ALWAYS

This book isn't just for families. This book is for young people who may be saving for a mortgage, for people moving out of their family home for the first time, for students living on tiny loans or bursaries, for the newly separated or divorced going it alone and living on a single income, for parents on maternity or paternity leave, for those facing redundancy or a career change. This is for anyone who has experienced life changes that have impacted them financially. Even if you only take away two or three practical tips, I guarantee that you will save money and start to see opportunities to live for less.

This book isn't just for now. This book is a reference to keep, to dip in to when you need to flex your budget. This book will help you face the inevitable financial challenges that life changes bring, with a sense of control. By practising what I preach, I have eliminated the fear and uncertainty that financial change brings. There is a solution to every problem if you have the right mindset to face it head on. You really never know what is round the corner.

THRIFTY TEMPLATES

LIVING BUDGET HEALTH CHECK PLANNER

The table is to be used as a guide to work out your cost of living based on your personal circumstances. The things that I have included are a pretty good starter for ten to steer you in the right direction. I have also included some additional blank lines as I realise that not all of our expenses and living costs will be identical.

What are you spending money on?	Current monthly cost	Costs that can't be changed	Monthly cost after changes	Key to find saving ideas
Rent/Mortgage				
Gas/Electric				
Water				
Council Tax				
TV Licence				
Secured loans				
Debt or loans including student loans, Klarna, etc.				
Catalogues				
Store cards				

THRIFT YOUR LIFE

What are you spending money on?	Current monthly cost	Costs that can't be changed	Monthly cost after changes	Key to find saving ideas
Credit cards				
Broadband				
Home telephone				
TV subscriptions				
Netflix				
Spotify				
Mobile phone contracts				
Life insurance				
Car insurance				
Pet insurance				
Children's Trust Funds				
Gym memberships				
Regular prescriptions				
Car maintenance				
Car fuel				
Car Tax				
Public transport to school				
Car parking				
Clothes & shoes				
School uniform				
Pet food				

THRIFTY TEMPLATES

What are you spending money on?	Current monthly cost	Costs that can't be changed	Monthly cost after changes	Key to find saving ideas
Pet medicines & flea treatment				
Hobbies & clubs				
Food				
Cleaning				
Toiletries				
Make-up & beauty				
Hairdressing				
Amazon Prime				
Amazon subscriptions				
Gaming subscriptions, e.g., Xbox Live				
Google app subscriptions				
TOTAL				

ENERGY AUDIT TABLES

I would recommend using these in conjunction with the Sust-It energy calculator available from the energy efficiency database website Sust-It. The unit process on the calculator is adjusted to correspond with any rises so you can always get an accurate view of exactly what your appliances cost to run. I have broken the tables down into type and added additional lines for extra appliances that you may have.

Kitchen			
Appliance	**Wattage**	**Cost per hour**	**Cost per 10 mins**
Kettle			
Hob			
Electric grill			
Panini/Toastie maker			
Air fryer			
Halogen oven			
George Foreman grill			
InSinkErator tap			
Toaster			
Pressure cooker			
Blender			
Slow cooker			
Extractor fan			

THRIFTY TEMPLATES

Utility room			
Appliance	**Wattage**	**Cost per hour**	**Cost per 10 mins**
Immersion heater			
Tumble dryer			
Dishwasher			
Washing machine			
Clothes steamer			
Iron			
Vacuum cleaner (plug-in)			
Vacuum cleaner (cordless)			

Entertainment			
Appliance	**Wattage**	**Cost per hour**	**Cost per 10 mins**
PlayStation			
X Box			
Nintendo Switch			
Plasma TV			
Sound bar speaker			
CRT TV			
OLED TV			

Appliance	Wattage	Cost per hour	Cost per 10 mins
Desktop PC			
Laptop			
Monitor LCD 17-inch			
Monitor LED 17-inch			
Wi-Fi Mesh system			
Sewing machine			
Halogen lightbulb			
Filament lightbulb			
LED lightbulb			
Charging smartphone			

Heating & drying			
Appliance	Wattage	Cost per hour	Cost per 10 mins
Gas boiler			
Fan heater			
Storage heating			
Oil-filled heater			
Halogen heater			

Appliance	Wattage	Cost per hour	Cost per 10 mins
Calor gas heater			
Open fire			
Dehumidifier			
Electric blanket (bed)			
Heated towel rail			
Heated clothes airer			
Heated throw			
Air purifier			

Beauty			
Appliance	Wattage	Cost per hour	Cost per 10 mins
Hairdryer			
Straighteners			
Tongs			

Bathroom energy costs October 2022		
Energy required to heat 1 litre of water: 0.4kWh		
Electric cost to heat 1 litre of water = 34p per kWh/0.4 = 0.85p per litre		
Gas cost to heat 1 litre of water = 10p per kWh/0.04 = 0.25p		
Gas		
Bath 80 litres		
Shower 6 litres per minute	5 mins/30 litres	10 mins/60 litres

WEEKLY & MONTHLY MEAL PLANNERS

If you don't have a computer or are not savvy with a spreadsheet, don't worry – paper meal planners do the job just as well. I have included both weekly and monthly meal planners, as I recognise that some folks will not have the luxury of freezer space for a big monthly shop and prefer to plan and shop weekly. As this is *your* budget and *your* plan, it needs to fit with your household habits and needs.

Weekly Meal Planner			
Day	Meal	Ingredients for shopping	Cheapest way to cook the meal
Saturday			
Sunday			
Monday			
Tuesday			
Wednesday			
Thursday			
Friday			

Monthly Meal Planner

Week One

Monday	Tuesday	Wednesday	Thursday	Friday	Saturday	Sunday

Week Two

Monday	Tuesday	Wednesday	Thursday	Friday	Saturday	Sunday

Week Three

Monday	Tuesday	Wednesday	Thursday	Friday	Saturday	Sunday

Week Four

Monday	Tuesday	Wednesday	Thursday	Friday	Saturday	Sunday

SHOPPING LIST

I like to organise my shopping list so that it roughly corresponds with the way things are laid out in the supermarket. This stops me from veering off course and mooching down aisles where I have no business being. I am easily distracted by the shiny offers and new product launches, so I have to stick to a list to prevent my head being turned by off-list items and fancy packaging. Throwing stuff in the trolley with wild aplomb is a sure-fire way to exceed your grocery budget, so a list that is put together based on your meal planner is an absolute must.

Protein – meat, fish, eggs & cheese	Total cost

Vegetables	Total cost

THRIFTY TEMPLATES

Carbohydrates	Total cost

Seasonings & sauces, etc.	Total cost

Frozen food	Total cost

Drinks	Total cost

SUPPORTING CHANGING HABITS & MINDSETS

The following templates are to be used in conjunction with Chapters 1 and 2. You may wish to copy these so that you have a ready supply to keep in a journal. These exercises, as with the budget planners, are not intended to be completed one time only. You wouldn't stop going to the gym and expect to stay toned and fit, and the same principle applies to maintaining a healthy mindset and relationship with spending. Think of these as exercises to maintain your fitness, attitude and feelings about living a contented thrifty life.

SEVEN STEPS TO SHOPPING SELF-AWARENESS

This exercise is to be used before you make a rash or impulse purchase. It is essentially a cooling-off tool that will make you more self-aware of your triggers for spending on non-essential items. Getting into the habit of repeating these steps when you are hovering over the "Buy It Now" button on an online shopping basket will equip you with insight into your inner saboteur; it will make you question your purchase and, in time, become second nature.

1	**What time is it?**
2	**How am I feeling?**
3	**Do I want it or do I need it?**

4	How will I feel if I do not buy this item?
5	How much use will I really get from this purchase?
6	How long can I live without it?
7	Do I still want to buy it?

THE HAPPINESS SCALE

This table is to be used to review your previous month's spending: how many purchases were essential, what bought you joy, where do you waste money?

Item	Cost	Type of purchase	Scale of 1–5 Happiness or Usefulness	Reason for score

FINAL THOUGHTS

I hope that I have convinced you that being thrifty isn't all sackcloth and ashes. I have enjoyed writing this book because I am passionate about helping people, and I like to think that I am doing my bit toward living sustainably. I also wanted to share my love of sniffing out juicy bargains and creative ways to live for less. I firmly believe that once you get your hustle on and start to thrift your life there is no going back. You can be confident that you won't be fleeced, seen off or shafted – and, before you know it, you will want to get the best value that you can for every penny of income that you bring into your home.

ACKNOWLEDGMENTS

ACKNOWLEDGEMENTS

For my mum and gran: two of the strongest women I have ever known, whose grace and gratitude have seen them through the toughest of times.

For my children, Archie and Daisy, who adapted to a heating-free winter with fortitude and resilience – never a complaint, never a groan.

And for Argos – because without our trusty electric blankets we all would have frozen.

FURTHER RESOURCES

Financial help and support

Where to go for up-to-date, free, impartial information, advice and guidance on debt.

www.stepchange.org

www.nationaldebtline.org

Food

As well as saving money, tackling food waste by using leftovers – whether they be from your own fridge or from local takeaways and restaurants – is a great way to eat for less. I have included a variety of food-related sites that cover everything from foodbanks to budget recipes to supporting reducing food waste below.

olioapp.com/en/

www.toogoodtogo.com/en-gb

www.trusselltrust.org/get-help/find-a-foodbank/

www.bonappetit.com/gallery/leftover-friendly-recipes

mysupermarketcompare.co.uk

www.trolley.co.uk

www.bbcgoodfood.com/recipes/collection/cheap-family-suppers-recipes

Cashback

These are my favourite and easiest-to-use cashback apps.

www.topcashback.co.uk

www.quidco.com

loyalbe.io

www.airtimerewards.co.uk

Online banks with interest and saving pots

These are my preferred online-only bank accounts for ease of application and use.

monzo.com/monzo-account/

www.chase.co.uk

Factory seconds

Below is a selection of online retailers offering factory seconds at great reduced prices. If you are looking for something specific or niche from a particular retailer I would recommend a quick google search of the particular retailer followed by the word "clearance" as they may just have their own outlet.

factorysecondsfurniture.co.uk

www.factoryseconds.co.uk

topbrandoutlet.co.uk

www.elekdirect.co.uk

www.argos.co.uk/events/clearance

Clothes

I have listed my most-loved online sources for preloved clothes. These are my favourites because they are either really easy to use, offer the best bargains or have a really nice community feel like Clobber Swap and Poshmark.

www.vinted.co.uk

poshmark.com/brand/Uk

clobberswap.co.uk

www.vestiairecollective.com

www.depop.com

www.bkinda.co.uk

www.nct.org.uk/get-involved/fundraising-activities/buy-or-sell-
nct-nearly-new-sales

NOTES

NOTES

NOTES

NOTES